Whose Child?

An Adoptee's Healing Journey
From Relinquishment
Through Reunion . . . and Beyond

KASEY HAMNER

TRIAD PUBLISHING
LA CRESCENTA, CA

Library of Congress Catalog Card Number: 99-95141
ISBN: 0-9674145-0-4

Printed in the United States of America

Published by

Triad Publishing
P.O. Box 8514
La Crescenta, CA 91224-0514

Phone/Fax: (818) 957-5526

Email: healingheart@earthlink.net

Website:
http://www.bookzone.com/bookzone/10001914.html

THIS BOOK IS DEDICATED TO . . .
All members of the
adoption triad--birth parents,
adoptive parents, and adoptees--and
all others whose life
has been touched
by adoption

Disclaimer

This book is about my personal experiences of growing up adopted—it is not intended to tell the story of any other individual. The ideas in this book represent merely my opinion—my selective perception and interpretation of my own experiences as an adoptee.

The events represented in this book are true and accurate to the best of my memory and knowledge, but the identity of the persons involved has been disguised to protect their privacy.

The names, dates, places, and all other identifying information have been changed. Any similarities to other persons or events is purely coincidental.

Acknowledgments

I owe a debt of gratitude to the following:

Tiffany Hauck, Betty Jacobson, and Virginia Iorio—my friends and assistants—without whose creativity, expertise, and dedication this book would not have been completed. Here's looking forward to book number two!

My greatest love and biggest fan (whom I have called Warren Edwards in this book), for his undying patience, love, and encouragement throughout this project and life in general. You are still the man.

My adoptive mother (Connie Hamner) for accepting the challenge of raising me as her own child. Thank you for supporting me in this endeavor, accepting that we did not always see eye to eye. Despite our differences, your dedication and efforts will never be forgotten.

My adoptive father (Pat Hamner) for listening to me ramble on about the joys and sorrows of being adopted, and for being my father in the truest sense—in the only way that matters.

My birth mother (Vanessa Sobel) for giving me life and answering my endless questions with love and kindness.

My birth aunt (Liz Geiger Butler) and birth grandmother (Elaine Geiger) for finding me. You both have been instrumental in changing my life for the better.

Also, my extended-family members and friends (Mark Geiger, Adam Sobel, Kimberly Hamner, Nathaniel Geiger, James Butler, Meredith Babcock, Rebecca Babcock, Jeffrey Daniel Sobel III, Rebecca Sobel, Amanda Sobel, Anne Hartz, Elizabeth Maverick, Auntie Mona Stewart, Michelle Mills, Pat Sobel, Simon Sobel, Autumn Sobel, Dennis Sobel, Todd Hamner, Peter Hamner, Mark DeFazio, Bernie Fanfield, Reza Serajena) for you have all played a large part in the molding of me.

And all my other friends out there—too many to list, but you know who you are—thanks for all your love and support while I was writing this book. I hope you realize what a difference you have made in my life and in this project.

Last, but not least, I thank all those who took the time to read my manuscript and gave precious feedback.

Contents

Introduction

My Opinion

Allow me to formally introduce myself. My name is Kasey Hamner and I was adopted in the closed adoption system in the late 1960s. I'm currently a school psychologist and a licensed educational psychologist who works with special needs children, many of whom, as luck would have it, are also adopted or have been abandoned in some way. The longer I am in the reunion process, the more fascinated I become with the topic of adoption and its lifelong effects on members of the adoption triad—birth parents, adoptive parents, and the adoptee. In my adult life I have channeled this fascination by reaching out to the adoption community in order to better understand the realities of adoption from all sides of the triad. I started an advice column on the Internet and went to support group meetings to learn how to deal with my own lifelong adoption issues and to hopefully help others heal from their pain.

My parents, both teachers and in their thirties at the time, adopted me because my adoptive mother wanted a girl after giving birth to two boys. My adoptive father, who was emotionally absent from my life until I reached adulthood, was not sure if he wanted a third child because his two biological sons were more than he could handle. Unlike the vast majority of adoptive parents, my adoptive mother did not suffer from infertility, and therefore never had to go through a grieving process like most adoptive mothers. She basically had nothing to lose. She wanted to create the perfect family and refused to risk the burden of carrying and bearing a child again only to be disappointed by what she felt would be the arrival of yet another son.

If you have previously read any books on adoption, then you may recognize me as a textbook, run-of-the-mill, garden-variety adoptee. I displayed all the classic symptoms laid out in the adoption literature. Although I am a classic adoptee, I wish to make the point that I was not raised in a typical adoptive home. While my adoptive parents attempted to provide a loving, safe, and nurturing environment in which to raise me, I felt I was treated differently than my brothers. I was molested by my adoptive brother and felt unprotected by my adoptive parents. In my eyes, my adoptive mother was extremely controlling and was unable to see me as a person separate from her. While on the outside we looked like the perfect family, I never felt that I belonged. The soul connection was missing.

I survived in my adoptive family by presenting a false self, the self I thought my adoptive mother so desperately wanted, until I couldn't pretend anymore. Growing up I did whatever I could to please my adoptive family, especially my adoptive mother. I was scared to death of my brother and I always looked for approval from my adoptive mother, which never came to my satisfaction. I wasn't a troublemaker. I looked like I had it all together. I was a petite, overachieving actress who appeared to have adjusted well to her adoptive family. But in reality I trusted no one and waited for the next person to abandon me as I felt my birth mother had done. Of course, I was not aware of this until I reached adulthood.

My personal experiences of growing up adopted, my conversations with other adoptees and members of the adoption triad, and my studies and work with abandoned children have all proved to me that there are many common threads running through adoptees' lives. The main issues that I see in others and have uncovered in my own life are fear of abandonment, self-sabotage, relationship difficulties, substance abuse, and an inability to trust and bond with others. In my case, I was never able to bond with my adoptive mother and I was only able to bond with my adoptive father after becoming an adult.

I sincerely appreciate the experts who have painted such an accurate picture of the other issues that adoptees also deal with, including loss, rejection, guilt/shame, grief, identity confusion, fear of intimacy, and control. I am here to illustrate how all those issues apply to me. The adoption literature often states that insecure attachments, common with adoptees, lead early in life to problems such as relationship difficulties, personality disorders, feelings of insecurity, and low self-esteem. My personal experience in these areas only adds to my conviction that I represent the typical adoptee.

Many books out there are feel-good stories that romanticize adoption as a fairy-tale answer to unplanned pregnancies or any other situation in which one chooses to relinquish a child. The reality of adoption is a far cry from the fantasies played out in so many fictional stories and movies that have the inevitable happy ending. In my opinion, adoption displaces not one, but two families. The reality of adoption affects adoptees, birth parents, adoptive parents, and all other relatives, both birth and adoptive. It is crucial that the adoption worker inform all members of the triad about the effects that adoption can have on the child, whether adopted in an open or closed system, or through a private, independent, or county agency. The feelings are real and the ramifications are extensive for all members of the adoption triad. Although the initial trauma of separation is detrimental enough, it is the ultimate secrecy of adoption that perpetuates the trauma of the adoptee more than anything else.

In addition to being plagued by secrecy—the hallmark of adoption—adoption is also one of the most misunderstood subjects. People generally don't want to talk about it. Legislators in favor of sealed records might answer my plea for open records if they knew more of the truths of how secrecy in adoption adversely affected my entire life.

Prior to my reunion I used to wonder when legislators would stop treating me like a perpetual child by refusing me access to my records, even if they revealed unpleasant information. The fact that I was placed in an adoptive home already told me that something unpleasant had already occurred. After all, women generally don't get pregnant just so they can celebrate giving up their child. I used to say to legislators, "Stop trying to keep me from my God-given right of knowing who my biological parents are and the circumstances surrounding my relinquishment."

In reunion, I still feel that no other adult has the right to decide what part of my life I should be allowed to know. When I made the decision to search, I was not a child. I was an adult with reasonable intelligence who should have been allowed to make my own decisions and deal with the facts of my own life as I saw fit. Now that I am in reunion, I can say with certainty that not knowing the truth was worse than dealing with the truth. It is my right to know my past and come to grips with it on my own terms. The atrocity is that laws had to be broken in order for me to learn the truth.

Back in the late 1960s, birth parents did not have any input in the future of their child. They were told to trust the agency's judgment, accept their rules, and agree to sealed records that precluded any contact with their child. The agency basically told them, "Get over it and get on with your life." The agency also told the adoptive parents to treat the adopted child as their own. They never told them that the child they were raising was a traumatized child who would probably have a different temperament and not be emotionally, physically, and spiritually the same as them. They didn't divulge that these differences would have deep-rooted, far-reaching effects. No one counseled the adoptive parents on how to deal with the inevitable challenges that arise when raising an adopted child. No one told them how many adoptees feel a nagging, ongoing loneliness and devastating feelings of rejection. No one told them that to an adoptee, separation from the birth mother feels like death. And just because a child can't remember the separation, it doesn't make it any less devastating.

Many adoptive parents still cannot comprehend that no matter how hard they try or how wonderful they are as guardians, they will never be able to take the adoptee's pain away. Today, thankfully, many birth parents have input in selecting the couple who will raise their children, and in some cases, as in open adoptions, are allowed to keep in contact with their children over the years. Also, there is now a plethora of information out there to help adoptive parents deal with the challenges of raising their adopted child.

Nevertheless, everyone in the adoption triad experiences loss and pain: The adoptee loses the birth parents and feels self-blame; the birth parents lose their child; and in most cases, the adoptive parents lose their dream of procreating. I should have always known my birth parents' identity, and my birth parents should have known my location and information about who raised me. Someone should have made my adoptive parents aware of the subtle yet significant issues they would face in raising an adopted child.

One way for us to educate one another is to have all members of the triad write their stories. I want to understand where other members of the triad are coming from, and I hope that by reading my story, you will understand where I'm coming from. We need to stick together and accept the choices, right or wrong, that we have made and the feelings those actions caused in ourselves and others. I have made many mistakes in my life and my relationships and have hurt others with the choices I have made. Fortunately, as an adult, I have been able to mend the relationships and have been able to heal from much of the pain that plagued me as a child. All of us must take the road less traveled and share the truth about our feelings and experiences concerning adoption. We must get the word out about how adoption affects each member of the triad.

I chose to call this book *Whose Child?* because it was the question I asked myself most of my life, until I was able to move past the pain and accept that I am the child of many and there is a divine reason that I am here. I am an adoptee who not only had to grieve the loss of my birth family, but also had to grieve the loss of a large portion of my adoptive family. Growing up, I felt confused and lost because I didn't know my birth mother and felt my adoptive parents were the enemy. I also never bonded with my adoptive mother. Now that I am an adult adoptee in reunion, my birth mother is still unable to connect with me as much as I had hoped or tell anybody outside the family that I am her daughter, and my birth father has chosen to relinquish me from his life—the ultimate fear I had when I was growing up.

In a nutshell, I have two mothers, neither of whom I felt was up to the challenge of parenting me. My birth mother was unable to parent me because of fear, and I felt that my adoptive mother was unable to stick with me when I stopped allowing her to treat me poorly. It wasn't until I took the first step in contacting my adoptive mother after two years of estrangement that I was able to accept that she did the best she could with the parenting tools and resources she had.

The baby picture of me on the cover of this book was taken at the adoption agency. My birth mother gave it to me after our reunion. This was the only picture, and the only physical remembrance of my existence, that my birth mother had of me until our reunion over five years ago when I was twenty-seven years old.

This book neither endorses nor opposes adoption. It simply relates my experiences, perceptions, and feelings about being adopted, from the time of infancy through the present as an adult adoptee currently in the post-reunion process. I did not write this to blame anybody. I understand the need for adoption as an option. I do not blame my birth mother because she gave me up. I know it was a hard decision for her, and most importantly, I know that she did not give me up for adoption to hurt me. Nevertheless, it *did* hurt me and this is just an account of my reaction to that hurt and how I dealt with it through the various stages of my life. Truthfully, I have a stupendous life filled with miracles, but in addition to this I have dealt with underlying issues that many others who have been touched by adoption also have experienced. If we can communicate openly with one another, we can have an increased level of acceptance about what most adoptees have felt, as I have, at various times in their lives.

I had written this book in my thoughts throughout my entire life, and once my reunion took place I was able to fill in the gaps with the truth, not fantasy. I was finally able to take my birth family down from the pedestal I had subconsciously placed them on while growing up. As a result, I have now decided to commit my story to paper. I tell my story of being lost and found. I tell my story of isolation and discovery. I tell my story of addiction and recovery. I tell my story of failure and success. I tell my story of reunion and post-reunion tragedies and triumphs. I tell my story of amazing coincidences and synchronicities—the spiritual and emotional connections between myself and my birth family, a very common phenomenon in adoption. Basically, I talk about living life on life's terms. I also recount the circumstances of my relinquishment as told to me by my birth mother and birth grandmother following my reunion, realizing of course that there's more than one side to every story. My goal in writing this book is not only to facilitate the healing of myself and other adoptees, but also to help all members of the adoption triad, and anyone else touched by adoption, to develop a better understanding of what it is like growing up adopted.

I do not claim to be an expert on adoption, only an expert on how my adoption affected me. I write this story as an adoptee who became a psychologist. Only after I began studying to become a psychologist was I able to see the blind spots in my own life and acquire some perspective, which has helped me immensely in my healing process. I hope that those who read this book will take my experiences, both positive and negative, and learn from them in order to develop a more compassionate way of dealing with the adoptee in their life. I especially hope that all members of the adoption triad who relate to a person or situation that I describe will realize the effects of their actions. For instance, if you are an adoptive parent, I hope that my experiences with my adoptive family will provide food for thought as you continue your quest to be the best possible parent to your adopted child. If you are a birth parent, I hope you consider all the variables when you decide to give up your child or to reunite.

I invite all members of the adoption triad, and those who love us, to read this story and see the truth in it so that we can better serve members of the triad in the future. I haven't written this book to gain your sympathy, only to write the truth as I perceive it. Please enjoy this book in the spirit it was written, as a vehicle to help me and others heal and grow.

Chapter 1

Separation

The date is October 12, 1967. Inside the hospital, air conditioners are keeping the rooms at a comfortable coolness. Fluorescent lighting glares off the white walls, draining all personality from the antiseptic surroundings.

In a birthing room, a young woman—a girl, really—lies upon a raised hospital bed. Despite the coolness of the air, sweat drops from her brow. She breathes deeply, eyes darting around the room in anxious anticipation. Then suddenly, it comes. Another contraction. She doubles over in pain. The drugs they shot into her veins barely deaden the turmoil as it boils deep inside her.

"Breathe," says a nurse, the one who holds her hand. "Breathe."

A moment later, the pain dissipates. The girl, only nineteen, leans back again. Her head feels dizzy from the pushing and breathing. Her legs, draped by a surgical sheet, lie wide open as she turns her head to the side. The sheet feels cool and clean against her cheek, wet from the sweat and tears. She looks to the closed door in hopes of catching a glimpse of him out there, the love of her life, the father of her child. But he is nowhere to be found.

He looked nonchalant that morning when she awakened him around five a.m., the first spasms of labor shaking inside her abdomen. She paused for a moment, admiring him, running her hand through his thick wavy hair before she awoke him. When he looked up at her sheepishly, his head still thick with sleep, she said simply, "The baby's coming," and he bolted out of bed.

"All right, let's get this over with!" he said. "I'll drop you off." Then he picked up yesterday's jeans from the floor, almost tripping as he stepped into them.

"It's all right," she said, slowing him down with her beautiful smile. She reminded him it was only the beginning, that they still had time. Even as she said it, she sighed to herself. There really wasn't any time. Not really.

Another flash of pain yanks her back to the present. Her whole body clenches tight, and before the doctor even tells her, she knows instinctively it's time to push.

"That's right," says the doctor, as she feels his hands against her skin. "One more time." The world goes black as she closes her eyes and pushes. "Again," he says, his voice steady as steel. He's seen this hundreds of times.

Darkness again, life brimming from her insides. His hands against her thighs, the nurse's hands in her own.

"Come on. You're doing great. Just once more."

With all she has, she pushes, and in a moment, in one unbelievable moment, the child is born. It is 3:07 in the afternoon.

How many times had she envisioned this moment in her mind over the last few months? The doctor, smiling broadly, would announce, "It's a girl!" and place the child, wet with newness, in her arms. She would open her eyes as the bliss of childbirth spread across her face. She would see the elated face of the doctor.

But not today. Instead all she sees when she wakes up from her drug-induced stupor is a flash of moving white as the nurse holding her baby exits the birthing room, leaving the young mother with an emptiness that surely could never be filled.

These facts surrounding my birth and pre-birth are as accurate as I can make them. I find names and dates easier, while other specifics often elude me. The stories of how I came to be, and the stories of those who loved me enough to create me and give me life, did not come to me across the dinner table as tales handed down by tradition. Neither were they secrets whispered in a private moment between grandmother and child, where history is passed on and a definition of self emerges. Because in the hospital room that October afternoon, my mother didn't hold me. No love passed through her fingers to the depths of my newly formed soul. Instead of making the unbreakable connection between mother and daughter—an event quite unlike any other phenomenon and one that can only be felt, not described—I was handed not to my father, nor to a proud family member, but immediately to a nurse who whisked me away to the nursery. My mother never held me, my parents never gave me a name. They gave me up and let me go. The door to life, having just opened for me, slammed shut before I had a chance to walk through it.

At the time of my relinquishment, the adoption agency's policy was to place all children given up for adoption into a foster home, regardless of whether another family had already agreed on a specific adoption. In accordance with this policy, all babies remained in foster care for their first three months of life to ensure their health and suitability for adoption. If the agency determined that the first foster family was unsuitable, they moved the child again, and perhaps again, until the three-month time period expired.

I have no record of who my foster parents were, or whether the agency placed me in more than one foster home. I will never know who held me, fed me, bathed or changed me for the first three months of my life. This part of my past haunts me, conspicuous by its absence. What sort of people let this new life into their homes, and bought the bassinet in which I lay at night? Against whose chest did my head rest while I cried, longing for the mother I wouldn't see for decades? What did they call me? What was my name? And why didn't they want me, either? Even if by some miracle of God I found out their names, they would mean nothing more to me than any other words scribbled in black and white. I have no memories to give those names a meaning. I doubt they'd remember me, one of many babies who cried, who came and went in a short period of time.

Pat and Connie Hamner adopted me on January 16, 1968. They already had two sons, Todd, who was six, and Peter, three. My new highly educated parents experienced great financial success. A newly completed home in the extremely affluent neighborhood of Beverly Hills, California, awaited me upon my arrival. For my new family, life looked good. The adoption agency told them the first three months of my life passed uneventfully, that I was "a happy baby with a winning smile." They assured my adoptive parents that I would make an excellent addition to their family.

I wonder how they knew of my so-called happiness. Had they asked the foster parents who had taken care of me during those first few months? However they gained this information, they must have portrayed me inaccurately. According to my adoptive parents, I was dangerously emaciated as a result of refusing to eat and I was a projectile vomiter from the moment I arrived. Because of a spastic pylorus, I couldn't keep anything down at all. A doctor friend of mine describes projectile vomiting as a reaction to great psychological stress and "a sign of impending doom." With this knowledge, my vomiting and refusal to eat could in no way be mistaken as the sign of a so-called "happy baby." Perhaps I was reacting to my mother's absence. My adoptive mother tried desperately to increase my weight by switching my milk from non-fat to homogenized, but her attempts proved ineffective.

According to the experts, however, nothing was wrong with me, despite the fact that I was difficult to comfort in addition to being deathly thin. Of course, they didn't realize I had recently experienced what would be the most traumatic experience of my life—the separation from my birth mother. I believe to this day that the spasms and vomiting were my body's way of reacting to this stress by refusing to hold anything down. I believe the projectile vomiting existed as a sign of defiance on my part, as if I had made a conscious effort not to eat, to refuse to grow and mature as the "happy baby" I knew I wasn't.

A pamphlet that came with my arrival, a sort of instruction manual for my care, directed my adoptive parents to hold me often. My new mother, who was not a very affectionate woman, may not have found it comfortable to do this as often as recommended. For reasons yet unknown, the bonding that is so crucial between mother and daughter didn't occur. I did not, could not, would not bond with Connie, the woman who had signed up to be my mother.

Some adoption literature defines the incredible resiliency of infants, citing their ability to adjust quickly and normally to foreign environments. I accept this on a certain level, as I know that a Chinese child adopted in America would naturally learn English and the other traditions and social behaviors of this culture. However, I vehemently disagree on a much deeper level. I don't see repeated projectile vomiting as a sign of resiliency to change. It is one thing to adjust to traditions and learn new languages, and quite another to adjust to the impossible, the absence of mother.

The finalization of my adoption occurred on November 30, 1968. Like most adoptions, the process took almost a year. This gives the agency time to determine the suitability and capability of the family to successfully raise a child not their own. The agency checks out the family and parents, makes surprise home visits, writes reports, and makes decisions that will affect the child's life profoundly. My adoptive family passed the tests with flying colors, and at the age of one year and one month, I legally became a Hamner. At one year and one month of age I was officially given a name—Kasey.

As the months passed into years, I became a permanent fixture in the Hamner household. For all intents and purposes, I was the daughter of Pat and Connie, the sister of Todd and Peter. From the outside, our family must have appeared perfect. We did all the things that perfect families did. We went to amusement parks, traveled, had birthday parties, and our family pictures displayed merriment and contentment.

I was about four years of age when I first learned that I was adopted. Due to my age-limited thought process and comprehension level, I experienced difficulty in understanding the full ramifications of being adopted. My parents followed the suggested guidelines as to when they should begin to tell me about the adoption, but really, they began to tell me long before I could possibly understand what they meant. They told me a story, one that seemed much more like a fairy tale, about how they went to the adoption agency and looked in crib after crib until they came upon my crib. When they discovered I shared the same birth date as Peter, my adoptive mother took this as some sort of sign. They said that the moment they saw me, they knew I was the little girl for them. They assured me that I was "chosen" and "special," and reminded me that not everyone gets to be chosen, as I had been. They told me to always remember that I am special because I was chosen out of a hundred or so prospects. My immediate reaction to this information was, "Hey, I didn't get to choose anything!"

They explained to me that my birth mother loved me so much that she gave me up for adoption so that I would have a good home. Even at that young age, this didn't make sense. After all, I would never give away my favorite doll, who I loved very much. I didn't think you gave away the things you loved, so their explanation confused me. They explained in terms as simple as possible that my mother didn't feel as if she could provide or be responsible for me. Words like "provide" and "responsible" meant little to me. I wanted my real mother, the one who would love me as much as I loved my favorite doll.

Each time my adoptive parents told me the "chosen" story, I wondered how many children they really had to choose from. What if I had cried too much in their presence, or hadn't smiled enough? Would they have passed me by for the cute and quiet baby in the next crib? What if I hadn't had the same birthday as Peter? And what happened to those other babies, the ones who weren't as precocious or quiet, the ones who weren't chosen? What happened to them? What was their fate?

Now that I possessed this information, I remember feeling a constant fear. Despite the insistence of my parents, I felt neither chosen nor special. Instead, I felt defective. I asked myself why my own birth mother didn't want me. Why was I *unchosen* by her? What flaws and imperfections in me drove her away? I dreaded those imperfections in myself. I began to tell myself that if I didn't succeed in all my endeavors, which at that time consisted of building the best sandcastle and reciting the alphabet flawlessly, they could send me away or give me back to the place I'd come from. From the moment I learned about being adopted, I strove to become the perfect little girl. Instead of feeling special, I felt like I should have been grateful—grateful to have things other children took for granted. I had a roof over my head, a family who seemed to love me, and I lived in a nice big house with a huge backyard and a panoramic view from every room. Most importantly, I wasn't sleeping in a tiny metal crib among hundreds of other babies awaiting their destiny. What more could anyone want?

After learning that I was adopted, I felt increasingly different and uncomfortable in the family. Having to share my bedroom with the maid magnified these feelings. I noticed I didn't look like any of my family members, and my brothers relentlessly teased me about it. My vivid imagination started to conjure up fantasies of my birth mother's identity, and why she had given me away. I told myself there was something wrong with me, that she must have been horrified by my ugliness, because what else do babies have going for them but their cuteness? I thought I was the ugliest kid on the block. I would often dream that she was driving by the house to check on me, or that she would come to the door at any minute to pick me up and take me home. Despite the hopes that I clung to, deeper fears haunted me. I imagined that if she did actually come by, she would take one look at my ugly, disfigured face and drive past, glad for the decision she'd made.

When I got up the nerve, I would ask my parents to tell me the "chosen" story again, always wondering if my birth mother got to choose who would raise me in her absence. Despite their assurances, I still didn't feel special. I used to ask myself questions like, "If I'm so special, why do I have to share my bedroom with the maid while my brothers have their own bedroom?" and "Why do I feel like such a freak?" When we were in public and the topic of my adoption came up, I went along with the "chosen" story by smiling proudly, but inside I knew that I was different and separate from everyone else. At other times, when fear prevented me from asking my parents about the adoption, I made up my own stories. I let my vivid imagination run away with me.

One night, at the age of five, it was the maid's night off and I was lying in bed. My mind was spinning a mile a minute about what sort of woman my birth mother was. Evening had turned into night, and I should have been asleep. Outside, rain poured over the ground. I could hear it running through the trees and dripping off the eaves. At times like this, thoughts of her comforted me. As I lay there in the dark, bundled up warm in my blankets, I slowly drifted off to sleep. But my slumber was interrupted shortly thereafter by the harsh voice of my eleven-year-old brother, Todd, ordering me to wake up. At first, I was confused and disoriented. I didn't understand why he was in my bedroom. Was something wrong? Was I in trouble? Was there a fire? Was he coming to get me out before the house burned to the ground? No. It wasn't any of those things. Later, it made perfect sense. This night became the first night of many, over a span of ten years, in which Todd sexually abused me.

Even at this young age, I knew inherently the inappropriateness of Todd's behavior, but I had no idea how to deal with it. Here I was, trying to be the perfect little girl, and that included doing whatever anyone else told me to do—especially Todd, who until that point I had always looked up to and admired. He and I shared a closeness that escaped his relationship with our brother, Peter. He had always played the big brother to me, and early pictures of us show his arm draped lovingly over my shoulder, big grins on both of our faces. He had always loved and protected me. Now his behavior confused and scared me.

I suppose as a way of justifying the situation, I assumed that because I was adopted, it wasn't really wrong that Todd abused me. I had some vague comprehension of social taboos against this sort of thing, and gleaned from that information that incest only occurred between family members tied by blood. While I still didn't fully appreciate the concept of adoption, I knew, if only in the most rudimentary way, it meant Todd and I were not truly brother and sister, that we had different parents. Therefore, perhaps it wasn't completely wrong, after all. I tried to convince myself that it was okay, perhaps to avoid believing the unthinkable. Even so, why did I feel so horribly damaged by what continued to happen?

Meanwhile, Todd was becoming a different person. The boy who had always been so easygoing and friendly started to change drastically. Over time, he became very violent and was expelled from various schools for out-of-control behavior. My adoptive parents didn't know what to make of his behavior and I, feeling like the main target of his anger, was scared to even look him in the eye. Sometimes his violence would result in the destruction of furniture or other property around the house. I can vividly recall one particular day when Todd threw his skateboard into my mother's favorite entertainment center. I watched in amazement and wondered what had happened to the boy who once loved me as his sister.

My memories from this time are very murky, but I remember Todd being sent away for days at a time, only to return with no change in his behavior. I was never really sure exactly where they sent him, and why my parents ever thought it was safe to let him back in the house again. What I remember mostly is that he went away and returned often. His conduct in and around our home became a whirlwind of destruction, and he caught me in the aftermath. His behavior and the person he'd become scared me to death.

I slowly learned to trust no one. I felt deceived by Todd's former brotherly affection early in our relationship as siblings, and later betrayed by the molestation. If he could trick me, steal my trust, and destroy it over and over again, how could I trust any other person I might come across in life? Besides, no one would believe me anyway, even if I could somehow muster the courage to tell them, so I decided to keep everything a secret.

When his violence sometimes caused me physical pain, I feared he would kill me. One day, as Todd raged against my mother, Peter and I looked on. I remember the baseball bat Todd held tightly in his clenched fists. As Peter tried to protect our mother, I stood there in front of him, crying hysterically. Todd swung the bat to hit Peter, and on the upswing he hit me square on the nose. I took this as a premonition of what else awaited me if I ever broke my silence.

Chapter 2

Coping

Directly after the molestation began, I turned to food for solace. I became a binge eater and a food thief. I secretly went into the kitchen at night while everyone else slept and took loaves of bread to hide in my room, even though they would often become stale and inedible. At five and six years of age, I prowled around the house like this in the dead of night. I knew from experience exactly which floor tiles and cupboards creaked, which doors not to open so the sound in the silent house wouldn't awaken anyone to discover what bizarre behavior was being perpetrated by such a young child.

I knew enough not to plunder recklessly through the kitchen and leave obvious trails and clues to my adventure. It was my goal that no one realize what I had been up to, again hiding what I perceived as behavioral imperfections in my life. I became artful at this sort of cover-up. If I wanted crackers, I would never steal a whole box or even a handful. Instead, I

27

would take six crackers from three different boxes so no one would notice any disappearance. I would stand at the freezer and eat ice cream directly from the container, but never from the top like everyone else. Instead, I would dig a hole through the ice cream with a spoon and dig out what I ate from the bottom, hollowing it out as I went along. I would steal candy from my brothers' room while they played outside, and hoard everything under my bed or in my closet. I became an insatiable food fiend, never satisfied by what I had or what I could get. I'd become very compulsive with food.

At the time, I never fathomed the reasons for my behavior. Stealing food and bingeing came natural to me; thievery became a normal behavior in response to what my body yearned for. The high of getting away with stealing the food complemented the thrill of feeding my obsession. All I knew for sure was that when I ate I felt joy, something I didn't often feel. Looking back I can remember the times I wasn't eating. I was bathed in fear and apprehension that I wasn't performing efficiently, that I was defective, that someone would find out what Todd was doing to me and I would be blamed. I lived in a world all my own where fear and imagination dominated my behavior.

Food numbed me. The act of eating detached me, if only for that moment, from the demons of my world and allowed me to experience happiness that would ultimately save my life as an escape route from madness. I got a strange but exhilarating sensation that I was going to get the best of Todd. I wasn't going to let

Todd know how afraid of him I was. Food filled a hole in my life left by a mother who had abandoned me and an adoptive family who I felt wasn't protecting me from their firstborn son. It did the one thing that nothing else could do: give me love. I shared my little secret with no one. It was mine and mine alone, and no one could take away how it made me feel. Not my parents, not Todd, not anyone.

At about age six, I began a successful acting and modeling career. My mother, having decided I had a great look for commercials, took me to a photographer, had a plethora of head shots done, and promoted me around town to Hollywood agents. One of the largest talent agencies at that time agreed to represent me and immediately sent me on a slew of auditions. At first my mother seemed to want this success more than I, but eventually the bright lights of Hollywood excited me just the same. I got my Screen Actors Guild card almost immediately when I was a stand-in on a television show and the principal actress was misbehaving. I was asked to step in, say a few lines, and as a result was permitted to pay five dollars and join the union.

Being an actress made me feel special. I suddenly had something my brothers didn't have and everybody in school knew that Kasey Hamner was a "movie star."

And even though I wasn't in a movie for a couple of years, my friends loved to say I was famous. I would go on auditions anywhere from one to four times a week. My mother would pick me up after school, and I would change my clothes in the back seat of the car on the way to the audition. We would show up at a room full of other children like me, with mothers like mine who fussed over hair and clothes hoping their child would be the one to get the part.

They'd give me the script for the commercial, and I'd sit in the room with all those other kids as we tried to memorize the lines with our parents so that we could regurgitate them believably in front of the casting director later that afternoon. We would have to wait anywhere from fifteen minutes to an hour and a half before someone called us to read lines in front of one to twenty people. The entire time, I hoped I would be the one chosen for a callback and eventually for the part.

At the auditions, rivalries inevitably occurred. I always competed against one particular girl named Beth who possessed features strikingly similar to mine. We looked so much alike that casting directors would often mistake one of us for the other. Sometimes I got the principal part, and she posed as my stand-in—and vice versa. Whoever got the principal role teased the other for only being the stand-in. Once I was the stand-in for Beth on a horror movie. The scene she was working on was a frightening reenactment of two intruders who come into the house and murder her parents. For some reason, she freaked out and couldn't finish the scene. So I got to step in and witness an intruder killing my parents in our home. In hindsight, the whole thing is kind of ironic. In the following years, I had several nightmares in which I dreamt my birth parents were dead, perhaps murdered.

I became moderately successful, and worked quite often. My petite stature enabled me to play characters that were much younger than me. It became clear that directors wanted older petite actresses, hopefully with more maturity, to play younger characters. I did many television spots, and national commercials for clients such as McDonald's, Sunkist, Fanta soft drinks, and Kellogg's. I also modeled, and got a small television role as a patient on a soap opera. At the age of nine, I got the part of a lifetime—I was in a feature film playing the daughter of one of the biggest actors of that time. While my mother treated my success like a business, I was ecstatic. Even when I got the part in the movie she wasn't able to show me that she was happy for me. But I felt like a star, like I was just a little bit better than everyone else. With each success, my mother found it necessary to remind me that I wouldn't be successful if it weren't for her. She would often tell me that I was indebted to her for all she had done for me.

Acting quickly became an additional solace in life. I loved it. It was a dream come true. I was so unhappy with who I was, and spent so much energy keeping secrets from my friends about the incest, my food obsession, and especially the fact that I was adopted.

But when I acted, I was actually paid to become someone else. In time, I could forget the differences between me and everyone else in my family, and I could forget about the incest for a while. I learned quickly that cute faces and pretty smiles in front of the camera prompted attention and accolades from others. Acting became the perfect way for me to be special so I wouldn't be sent back to the agency from which I had come.

By the time I was ten years old, still bingeing in secret, I was well into a life of dieting enforced by my mother. She felt that I was too chubby for television, and as a result of my continued success in acting, she became obsessed with what I ate. "The thinner, the better" was her motto. I have to admit I was putting on a few pounds with all my bingeing, but my distorted body image led me to believe that I was huge. My mother forbade me to eat certain foods, especially candy, and weigh-ins became a weekly ritual. It seemed that my mother, a pack-a-day smoker, got more strict with my food intake every time she tried to quit smoking. I hated her for that. She would watch me eat to make sure I didn't eat one bite too many. When I was on location she used to remind my guardian that I was forbidden to eat any food off the catering truck. When she dressed me in frilly dresses, I would purposely stain them so I would have to take them off.

My mother always wanted me to look my best in public, while I aspired to be a tomboy as much as possible. I felt comfortable in a worn-out pair of jeans and tennis shoes.

In hopes that I would enjoy playing a musical instrument, my adoptive mother rented a piano and paid for weekly lessons. I hated the piano. I despised it so much that I would pretend to be worse than I really was. I would purposely forget the chords and the basic scales just so she would become convinced that I would never turn out to be a concert pianist. I sensed her disappointment but I didn't care.

Todd continued to abuse me whenever the maid had the night off, which was typically about three nights a week, and I began to hate myself more and more. I thought over and over again about telling someone about Todd, but couldn't seem to bring myself to do it. Since I was too afraid to tell someone, I felt determined to exhibit some behavior that might tip off others to what was happening to me—as if someday something would actually tip off my parents that their beloved firstborn was molesting me. At one point I pretended I had asthma. I would purposely breathe laboriously and hope my parents would notice. I prayed that someone would see the pain in my heart.

I even went so far as to ask my mother to put a lock on my bedroom door, but since she had no idea about the horror I was enduring, she said no. She didn't even ask why. Part of my fear about telling stemmed from the belief that Todd would kill me and in some inescapable way I could only blame myself for all that had happened. When I think back, I am amazed that asking my mother for a lock on my bedroom door didn't send up a huge red flag. I suppose that was when I really understood how alone I was, that my parents were oblivious to the goings-on in my life. Intellectually I could understand their preoccupation with Todd, since they were constantly running back and forth to jail and Juvenile Hall, but in my heart I was thinking to myself, "Hey, what about me? I'm dying over here."

Questions about my birth mother arose more and more often for me. It seemed the more time passed, the more anxious I grew to discover her story, as if it would somehow redeem me from the life I had lived and allow me to start again with a blank slate, snow white after the things that had already dirtied it. I began to ask questions like: What did she look like? How much did I resemble her? The only problem was that nobody could answer me. Sometimes I caught my own reflection in a mirror and stopped to look more closely. I examined my own eyes, nose, hair, mouth, smile, and body. Were any of them like hers? Did I walk like her, talk like her, laugh like her? And if I didn't find her soon, would that part of her, that individuality that made me so perfectly hers, somehow melt away?

I started to feel bad about my body. I looked nothing like my thin, perhaps anorexic mother, and this realization made me think something must be wrong with me. Next to her I felt fat, even though I was never more than ten pounds overweight. My father used to proudly announce to the family members who knew of my adoption how pleased he was that I resembled him. If you had to choose from the entire family, he was the only one I shared a few physical characteristics with. It was a sweet gesture on his part, but I didn't find it comforting at all. Rather, it perpetuated the way I felt different and apart from other members of my family. My friends and other people who did not know of my adoption would often comment on how they could see the resemblance between my father and me. He and I would laugh, but later I would roll my eyes in dismay, glad that he didn't reveal my horrible secret, that the resemblances were nothing more than coincidence.

As I approached my teenage years, the obsessions about why my birth mother had given me away increased and became more graphic. Perhaps someone had raped her. Would I want to know the answer to that? Could I deal with being the result of a violent crime against my mother? Would that somehow also be my fault? Or perhaps my dreams of a pristine mother were overrated. Had it only been a one-night stand? Had she stumbled home drunk one night, or to a sleazy motel with some man she'd picked up in a local dive? Did she know the father? Was he good to her? Did he care, or was he gallivanting around with the boys, bragging about the girl he'd banged at the bar last night? I tried to convince myself that my parents couldn't have been married, because if they were married, they wouldn't have given me up. Married women don't give up their children. My greatest hope was that they loved each other; my worst fear, like the nightmares I sometimes had, was that my parents were dead.

After projecting all of the possible bad things that could have surrounded my birth, I invariably went back to loving my birth mother, unconditionally, regardless of her abandonment of me. I wondered mostly about where she lived, and whether or not she thought of me as often as I thought of her. On holidays and birthdays I agonized over whether she missed me or not, because I certainly missed her. Most importantly, I desperately wanted my birth mother to know all that had happened to me so she could find me and take me away from it all.

I began to cry out for attention in any way I could. After years of keeping my shameful adoption a secret, I began to tell some of my friends. This was very serious business for someone like me. Being adopted was a huge secret, privileged information, and a friend would have to prove their loyalty to me and promise not to tell any other living soul my horrible secret. Most of my friends laughed at my seriousness and said it was no big deal. It angered me that they didn't understand the severity of it all. Couldn't they see how different I'd convinced myself I was?

In truth, I was jealous of them all. My friends looked so much like their siblings and parents, and got along with their mothers. I knew I could never experience such bliss. They took it all for granted. Meanwhile I searched endlessly, on buses and in banks, in line at the movies, and on street corner after street corner, for someone who looked vaguely like me. How long would it be before I would discover my own eyes, my own expression, my coloring and blood in the innocent face of another as they passed by?

The summer of my thirteenth year, my parents decided to vacation in France for three weeks. From the moment they told us about their plans till the time they actually left, I spent weeks in sweaty nervousness over the thought of their prolonged absence. All of a sudden, Todd would have no one to keep him in line. I somehow knew this would become a problem for me. I never thought I could be so hopeful that my parents would return home, soon and safe. When they left the country, they left me alone with Todd, Peter, and the maid.

It was a typical southern California summer that lured us outside for most of the days. Despite my fear of Todd, who was now nineteen and a good deal larger than me, my mother's absence left me free, if only for a short time. I could finally relax and not worry about what she might do or say that left me feeling insignificant. A few days after my parents left, nothing had happened with Todd, and I began to let my guard down. Perhaps everything would be all right. Maybe I had overreacted in the past. After all, adopted or not, he was my brother. He couldn't possibly intend to harm me now.

One afternoon, Todd and I were relaxing by the pool in front of the house and swimming in the scorching afternoon sun. Nothing felt better on a hot day. The maid was nowhere to be found. Todd and I splashed about, wrestling in the pool, when all of a sudden he grabbed my head and shoved it under the water. I tried to break loose and surface, but he held me down. At first I thought he was just playing, as I could hear him laughing, but when I ran out of air and began sputtering beneath the surface of the pool, I realized it was no joke. Todd was trying to drown me.

By kicking and flailing around, I managed to push my head out of the water for air. I was crying hysterically and screaming so that someone, anyone, would hear me, only to be shoved underneath the water's surface again. Later, he would claim I was laughing. At twice my size, Todd continued to push my head under, again and again, deeper and deeper. He took breaks once in a while and let my head up so I could choke in a necessary breath of oxygen before he plunged me into the depths once again.

Suddenly someone dragged me from the pool and laid me down on the hard cement of the deck. It was the paramedics. A neighbor, hearing my screams, had called an ambulance. I coughed up a lot of water and had trouble breathing. They rushed me to the hospital with water in my lungs, and I had to stay there until my parents returned from France two weeks later.

Ironically, I loved it in the hospital. That's the honest truth. I wholeheartedly embraced the place that so many other children feared. I made friends with all the nurses, and they would bring me toast whenever I rang the nurse call. The antiseptic white of the hospital made me feel clean, and the attention I received made me feel mysteriously special, in a way I had never quite felt before. Most of all, I felt safe there. It's sad to think I felt more at peace in the hospital than I ever had at home. I knew Todd couldn't harm me there. I had temporarily escaped his ever-present reach, if only for a while.

When I came home from the hospital, my mother immediately weighed me. I remember weighing two pounds over what she felt was acceptable. To my mother, this meant I was grossly overweight. She increased the strictness of my diet in an attempt to get rid of the apparent damage the hospital food had caused. Even after the attempted drowning incident, my mother continued to obsess about my weight and appearance and my father continued to be wrapped up in my brothers' problems. I felt so hurt and disappointed. I had built up in my head that my hospital stay could turn into a good thing, that they would finally see what harm Todd was causing me, and everything would change. But nothing did. In my eyes all I could see was that they didn't care that their firstborn son had put me in the hospital, that he had attempted to drown me. I knew at that point that they couldn't possibly love me, and nothing I could do, no amount of weight I could lose, would ever change that. The day I came home from the hospital was the day I turned against my adoptive parents for good. I told myself that if they weren't going to be there for me or protect me, then I wasn't going to try to be the good daughter they had hoped for thirteen years earlier.

Meanwhile, my brothers constantly caused trouble and broke their curfew. Whenever the maid was off, they used to bang on the sliding glass door of my first-floor bedroom in the middle of the night so I would let them in. My mother had told me in no uncertain terms not to let them in. She said they could sleep outside if they missed their curfew. Needless to say, they missed curfew nightly, and there they'd be, in the middle of the night, banging on that door and scaring the hell out of me. Therein lay the dilemma: Would I let them in so I could go back to sleep, or would I listen to my mother? In the end, I always opened the door, mostly because they threatened to beat me up if I didn't, and Todd already frightened me—for obvious reasons. By this time, I didn't care. I felt I was on my own.

As a teenager, I felt as if I was treated like a slave in my own home. While my brothers were constantly out getting into trouble, sometimes even with the police, I stayed at home and was responsible for the household chores. Now that I was old enough to do chores, my parents no longer employed a maid and I was responsible for almost everything—the cleaning, the laundry, and the yard work—as if I were now the hired help, both maid and gardener. My mother instructed me to keep the house immaculate. She would periodically do a "dust check" with her fingers. If she saw anything she considered less than perfect, she would have me do it all over again, and ground me in my bedroom for the night.

I remember listening to my neighborhood friends outside in the warm sun, riding their bikes or playing baseball in the street. I hated that I had to stay inside, doing the chores, and thought how unfair it was that my brothers got away with refusing to help out. I was told to finish everything before she'd allow me to go out with my friends. The only problem was that I never finished the job to her satisfaction.

Generally, I felt as if I had to beg my mother to let me go out with my friends. I used to pray that she would leave the house so that I could ask my father if I could go out with my friends. I knew he was more permissive and would let me do what I wanted. He would always ask me if I finished my chores for fear that if I hadn't, we would have to experience the wrath of my mother. I would show him the chores that I completed and we would both be satisfied with my performance. My mother, however, was rarely content and I would be instructed to come home early to redo them.

My mother started to keep a list of "misdemeanors," a record of all my wrongdoings, so that reasons for punishment would pile up over time. I remember telling my friends what kind of things I had done wrong, and they would laugh at how ridiculous it was. For instance, I didn't hang the laundry up perfectly, or my dusting didn't pass the white-glove test.

My resentment and hatred toward my mother grew every time she tried to control what felt like my every move. As long as something remained on the list, she would have a reason to say no anytime I wanted to go out with my friends. More often than not, I'd want to go over to a friend's house, but would have to stay home as punishment for failing a dust check weeks before. The misdemeanor would then be checked off the list, and she would add new ones at the bottom the next time I did something wrong.

This infamous list became longer and longer, and I ingeniously devised a way to work off the punishments that had built up. I decided I would make up social engagements so that she could "punish" me by not letting me go, thus allowing me to knock a misdemeanor off the list when I really didn't have anywhere to go in the first place. Unfortunately, she sometimes surprised me and said yes when I had made something up, at which point I would have to call up my friends and explain what had happened so they could come pick me up and get me out of there. Even though my friends were used to hearing detailed stories about my strict mother, I used to drive them and their parents crazy with all my shenanigans. I can recall countless times when one particular set of parents would begrudgingly pick me up and we would discuss how absurd my mother was behaving. I even had several parents jokingly tell me they would be glad to adopt me, just to get me out of the house.

When I made mistakes, I felt as if I had committed a serious crime. When I spilled milk or had some sort of accident, my mother would get so upset with me that I would feel like a complete idiot. I became afraid to screw up, to make even the most minute error. Unfortunately, this nervousness only resulted in more mistakes. I thought back to when my parents told me that my birth mother had given me away because she loved me. Now I knew that love meant abandonment. After all, I felt that my parents, who were supposed to love me, abandoned me emotionally every day—my mother by treating me like a slave and controlling my every move, and my father by allowing it.

Icontinued to act and I found myself with a substantial number of modeling jobs. Seeing how successful I was, my parents tried to involve my brothers in acting, but it didn't pan out for either of them. Once again, I felt secretly superior. In spite of everything, I was the one who could act, the one who could survive. I was the creative one, the cute one, and they were nothing.

Although I lived in a high-class neighborhood, I felt impoverished. I was made to wear hand-me-downs from my brothers, even old underwear of my mother's. My clothes embarrassed me. While my friends were wearing the in-style jeans, I was wearing my brothers' old corduroys. I saw this as just something else that set me apart from my friends and every other normal person in the universe.

I began to spend more and more time away from home with my friends. I never wanted to bring them over to my house because they used to tell me that they never felt welcome. My mother wouldn't allow me or anyone to sit on the new couch, and there was never any junk food to haul out in front of the TV for an afternoon of girl talk with sticky fingers. I tried to stay away from the house as often as I could.

I grew more and more afraid of Todd, and I dealt with him by avoiding contact with him as much as possible. I even ran away a few times, but never managed to get farther than my neighbor's closet. Sometimes I would hide under my girlfriend's bed and think seriously about staying there indefinitely. She would bring me food and keep me company. It was a fun game with serious implications. When her mother found out, she forbade her daughter to be friends with me anymore and claimed I was a bad influence on her. Time would show she was probably right.

My food-stealing and bingeing escalated as a teenager. When my mother discovered I stole food from our own kitchen, she began to lock the cupboards and tied string around the knobs so I couldn't get in. After she locked up every morsel of food in the house, she was confident that I would lose the few extra pounds I was carrying. Little did she know, I always found a way to get food. I eventually stole food from stores, not just from home. In school, other kids dared me to go to the grocery store up the block and steal candy bars for them. I would sneak off campus at lunch, scared to death that I'd get caught, but stubborn enough not to shy away from a serious dare. My concern for what everyone else thought of me always outweighed the fear of danger or punishment. After I filled my pockets with chocolate and licorice, I would return to school and spill the loot out before the wide eyes of my friends. At last I was a hero, and I could earn friendships this way.

Shoplifting became a regular pastime for me. On the weekends, I would walk from my home a mile and a half uphill to the local mom-and-pop grocery store, steal ten candy bars, and eat them on the way back home, throwing the wrappers in the bushes along the way. That way, no evidence existed to spur punishment from my mother. It seemed I always stayed one step ahead of her plans to make me as slender as she.

I even ventured into the cupboards of friends when I visited their homes and would sneak food to hide for later. I stole the good parts out of schoolmates' lunches because the cottage cheese and sliced apple my mother gave me was never enough. To this day, one particular person still remembers me as the one who used to steal her cupcakes.

At fourteen I was finally able to find something that I could use against my mother. When she would punish me or lock up the cupboards, I would tell her that I was going to find my "real" mother and leave her. I would tell her that I knew she didn't love me and that it obviously wouldn't mean anything to her if I left. The truth was, I missed my birth mother so much that I felt engulfed by that pain. I cried myself to sleep at night and prayed for her to find and rescue me. My birthday, a day that is supposed to be celebrated, only reminded me of my loss. The older I got, the worse my birthdays became. The parties my parents allowed me to throw could never cover up those emotions as we ate cake and played games to mark the day my birth mother had given me up for adoption.

The summer of my fourteenth year, I begged my mother to let me go away to camp. For some reason she did not want me to go, but thankfully my father decided it was best for me to go. I remember feeling so happy that I was going to get away from her. While I was at camp I hoped that my birth mother would somehow know I was there and would come and pick me up. Maybe she would be one of the camp counselors there! While the rest of the kids were experiencing homesickness I experienced elation. When it was time for me to go home, I have vivid memories of myself standing at the bus terminal, waiting for the bus to pick me up and take me home. There was only one problem: I didn't want to go home. I was crying hysterically, begging and pleading with the camp counselors so I wouldn't have to go back to that place where I felt so unloved, unwanted, and afraid. I wanted to stay at camp forever and water-ski, horseback ride and jump off the platform into the beautiful lake below. My friend who came with me didn't know what to do with me. She couldn't understand why I didn't want to go home. She was eager to go home like the rest of the kids. And while they were all experiencing joy at returning home, I went into a depression.

Looking back I am amazed that the counselors didn't find it odd that a fourteen-year-old girl was crying hysterically because she didn't want to go home. Why didn't they ask, "What is it that she doesn't want to go home to?" Nevertheless, I returned home where I was greeted by my mother, still upset at me for going away in the first place.

I'm convinced I could never have endured my childhood if not for the presence in my life of certain

individuals I came to believe could only have been
sent by God. We sometimes find our serenity in places
we could never anticipate, and so I found
mine—rainbows sparkling in the tumultuous storm of
my childhood. Without them, I surely would have
withered out of existence under the strain of enduring
the strictness of my mother, the sinister hands of my
brother, and the never-ending criticism I fed myself.

Elizabeth, my adoptive grandmother on my
mother's side, quickly became one of the people I grew
to love the most in life. She possessed everything I
admired, and everything I could ever hope to become.
A beautiful woman, she had been a small-time actress,
and sometimes sang show tunes from the films she had
appeared in. At one time, she had received offers of
contracts from MGM, Warner Bros., and other great
Hollywood studios, but the prospect of fame and
fortune hadn't interested her. I used to tease her by
saying that if only she had accepted those contracts and
become rich and famous, I would surely have enjoyed
success at the studios through nepotism. When she
heard this, she laughed in that musical way she had,
and I loved her even more.

Elizabeth was my favorite moviegoing companion.
I used to spend weekends over at her house, and we
would cook, go to the movies, and eat popcorn. When I
was with her, I felt like I lived a normal life in a place
full of love where someone appreciated me for my true
self. I could stop acting in front of Elizabeth, who
treated me no differently than she treated Todd and

Peter, her biological grandsons. It felt like Elizabeth didn't even know or care that I was adopted, that we didn't share the same blood.

I never doubted that she loved me. She told me all the time. She also told me how proud she was of me, words that sounded warm and foreign to my ears. It felt as if I could never do anything to impress my mother, no matter how well I behaved or how good my grades were. Yet I always impressed Elizabeth. With her, I didn't have to be anyone but myself.

Elizabeth became my confidante, someone to whom I told my deepest, darkest secrets—everything except the incest. I don't know why I didn't tell her about what Todd was doing to me. Perhaps it was because deep down I still felt I was somehow to blame, and even though I knew she loved me, her affection for me wasn't reason enough to show her my ultimate perceived imperfections. To my mother's chagrin, I would call Elizabeth time and again and complain about how she treated me. I remember asking her why my mother didn't love me, and if it was because I wasn't her "real" daughter. She would try to convince me that my mother loved me, and I would respond with, "Why doesn't she act like it? Why doesn't she ever tell me she loves me?" On many occasions she attempted to talk to my mother about her parenting.

What I remember most about her is how she made me laugh. She would come to the house and we would sunbathe by the pool. She would sing her show tunes and tell me stories about her life. Of course, perfection eluded even Elizabeth. She frequently had a drink in her hand and a cigarette dangling from her lip with lipstick encircling the filter, just like all those glamorous movie stars I had seen on the big screen. At family events, someone would always water down her liquor, but she always found a way to get all that she needed. All in all, I hoped that I would grow up to be like her, so gracious, so warm that she could make even the most uneasy outsider feel comfortable in her presence. All it ever took was her touch or her smile to wash away whatever bothered me.

One day when I was about ten, I was grounded in my bedroom, pretending my room was a bookstore. I would go around and put price tags on all my books, then ring them up at my pretend register. I was well into totaling up a hundred-dollar tab when someone knocked on my door. When I opened it, I was surprised to see Elizabeth standing there, a beautiful dog in her arms. She had rescued her from the pound as a gift for me. Once my parents begrudgingly agreed to let me keep her, I named her Sandy.

Sandy was a cockapoo, half cocker spaniel and half poodle. I fell in love with her instantly. Before long, Elizabeth showed up again with a second dog. This one was also medium-sized, a basenji. The second dog pleased my parents much less. My father felt one would suffice, but Elizabeth refused to back down. She begged him relentlessly until he gave in and allowed me to keep him. I named my basenji Sharka.

Sharka and Sandy were the greatest dogs ever, a perfect pair to protect and comfort me in the times when I couldn't escape the house for some peace of mind. I did everything with those animals—I slept, played, and cried with them. When my mother grounded me in my room for slamming a door, I would dress the dogs up and pretend they were people. The three of us plotted together against the rest of the world.

I related to Sharka as one might to a human being. He had been abused by his previous owner, and he came to us frightened of people, especially men. He got tense and skittish around my father and my brothers. In fact, he hated Todd instantly, as if he knew about the things Todd was doing to me. Perhaps he did know, since he was often in the bedroom while Todd molested me.

Like me, Sharka sometimes acted wild and rebelled against the family, only in a far more overt way. When we left him to roam free in the house while we were out, he became very destructive and would eat the wooden molding off the baseboards and chew up the drapes. He would howl incessantly while we were gone and the neighbors would complain. We even had to put electrical current on the fence that surrounded the backyard so he wouldn't jump over or dig beneath it.

I envied the way Sharka retaliated against everyone in that home. He achieved payback I could only dream of doing, since I knew how badly my parents would punish me if they were ever to return home and find me destroying everything in sight. Anger about life filled me to the brim and destructive thoughts of this nature certainly crossed my mind more often than not. Ultimately, I knew exactly how Sharka felt. I knew what it was like not to accept the family that had adopted you.

My aunt Mona, my mother's sister, was another soul mate in the family. I affectionately called her "Auntie Mona," and she loved me unconditionally. She was always struggling with her weight and, like Elizabeth, had a drinking problem. Mona seemed to enjoy spending time with me as much as I loved spending time with her. She listened to me with compassion and understanding in her heart, just like Elizabeth, especially when I divulged the problems I experienced with my mother. Mona assured me that my mother loved me very much but lacked the ability to show it. I could never believe it after all I had experienced, but I certainly believed that Mona loved me, as I so completely loved her.

Mona lived a hard life. In addition to being a heavy drinker, she was a two-pack-a-day smoker. At the age of twenty-five she was diagnosed with ovarian cancer and at age forty, the cancer had spread to her breasts and lungs. In spite of losing a lung, she continued to smoke. And despite pleading from myself and our entire family, she still continued to smoke after losing half of her remaining lung. She went through countless divorces and had terrific financial difficulties.

Notwithstanding her problems, Auntie Mona always managed to take me to places like Sea World, where we would spend the day together and laugh until long after the sun sank beneath the ocean. We also sunbathed together and chatted by the pool like two schoolgirls, even though she was old enough to be my mother. She told me I was beautiful, and that I could attain whatever goals I set for myself. Little by little, I began to believe her.

I thought with certainty that I could survive life if only I had Sharka and Sandy by my side, and Elizabeth and Mona close at hand. Barely a teenager, I was sure things could never get any worse. My best survival instincts were bingeing, stealing, and acting. Well, everyone has to have something.

Throughout my schooling, I excelled in all my academics. I studied hard to learn things that interested me, and continued toward what I perceived as perfection so I wouldn't disappoint my parents. The fear that I would be sent back into a vague nothingness if I didn't live up to their expectations for an adopted child did not dissipate as I grew older. Though I knew things beyond the scope of other kids my age, I couldn't see beyond my fears of rejection. And so, these fears drove me to succeed and improve with every waking breath.

My strong study habits as a student allowed me
other benefits in life. They made it easy for me to catch
on to other endeavors. Not surprisingly, as I became a
better student, I became a better thief. I continued to
steal as I moved into high school, behavior that now
seems a stark contrast to the successful student image I
portrayed. I didn't just steal food now. I moved on to
other things like shoes, purses, or anything else I could
get away with. But food continued as my primary urge,
and I would stop by the store after school and shoplift
my daily supply of candy bars. I'd slip out of the store
unnoticed, high on the rush of my thievery and the
thought of the sugar high that was to come. From there,
I'd hop on the bus to the local library where my parents
picked me up at the end of their workday. Signs strictly
forbade food in the library, but as always, I had to eat. I
would sit in a back corner by myself, huddled over a
pile of books as I did my homework, and sneak bites of
candy into my mouth. My eyes would dart around,
anxiously searching for someone who might notice me
and turn me in to the library police.

The library closed at five o'clock, but oftentimes my
parents were unable to pick me up until around six. I
was told to wait for them outside on a street corner. As
the year wore on into winter, it would be dark when the
library closed. I waited for my parents to come, praying
that maybe they'd arrive early for once so I could get
out of the cold. It frightened me to wait for them in the
dark when homeless men wandered around the same
street corner asking me for spare change. Sometimes I

sat on a fire hydrant on a busy street corner a mile from
school, in front of a mortuary, because there were no
benches. I'd get so scared waiting for my parents that
I would begin to wonder if they were really going to
come and get me at all. I hated them for that. I felt
abandoned again, as if one day they might just not
show up to get me at all, and then what would I do?
I even contemplated running away, this time for good.
As I sat there on the fire hydrant or on a cold bench,
waiting for them to arrive, I felt less like a human being
than usual. I didn't feel like a daughter or a part of their
family, but rather like one last errand on a long list for
the day, their last "pickup" before they headed home.

Birthdays continued to be a source of upset for me.
They served as a constant reminder of the day I'd been
abandoned by my birth mother, and I would usually
spend the week prior to my birthday in a state of what
I know today as depression. I began to obsess that my
birth parents were dead, not just wonder as I had
before. I even convinced myself that my adoptive
parents had told me they were dead, though of course
they never did. When the pain got unbearable, I wished
I had never been born.

On my fifteenth birthday, Peter and I had a combined
party, as we shared the same birth date. Peter turned
eighteen that day. As usual, Todd hadn't returned home
by the time dinner started. We didn't know at the time
that he was out drinking, but it wouldn't have
surprised any of us. At twenty-one, Todd drank and
used drugs heavily. This particular night, his drinking

caused him to speed down the street as he attempted to get home for the birthday dinner. Because he was drunk, he found himself unable to stop in front of our house. Instead, he swerved toward our next-door neighbor's house and drove through their walled fence, finally bringing the car to a stop in the middle of their pool.

He somehow crawled out of the car and dragged himself into the house. He reeked of booze and his dip in the pool had left him soaked and waterlogged. We were all gathered around the dinner table when he came in like that, and were shocked to see him in this state. I wondered what would happen next. You could have heard a pin drop. No one knew what to say. Todd walked around the table to where I sat, leaned over from behind me, and whispered into my ear in a raspy voice, "Happy Birthday, Kasey." My skin crawled. I could smell the alcohol on his breath and feel the hot wetness of it on my neck.

He still scared me to death. The molestation had continued from week to week and I had never said a word to anyone. My fears of both imperfection and Todd prevented me from telling anybody. But today I'd finally had it. He'd ruined my birthday party, and once again I felt humiliated. I never forgave him for the scene he caused that day, and that night I decided to tell my parents about the molestation.

I somehow knew that my mother would never accept the truth about Todd. Still, what did I have to lose? If things continued the way they were, I would disappear into nothingness, as I lost a piece of myself day by day. I had many things to consider when I decided to bring this up to my parents. After all, I would have to admit that I was no longer pristine, the perfect adopted daughter. Suddenly and thankfully, my desire to finally tell my parents about the molestation far outweighed my fear that Todd would harm me.

It was a Saturday morning. That much I can remember. I had decided to run the story by Peter first to see how he reacted and to get his opinion on how I should tell my parents about Todd's abuse. I'm not sure why I chose Peter to confide in, as he had taunted me for most of my life. He loved to point out that I didn't look like anyone else in the family, and made fun of the fact that I was flat-chested and shorter than everybody else. He enjoyed teasing me about the fact that I wasn't developing like my other girlfriends and that my friends and family members towered over me. In fact, he frequently found it necessary to tell "short people" jokes whenever I was around. Even though I knew he wasn't the most sensitive brother in the world, I needed to finally confide in someone. Though I knew Todd had betrayed me as a brother, I hoped Peter could rise to the challenge and support me. In spite of what I knew about Peter, his insensitivity and self-centeredness, his reaction surprised me. He laughed at me. I had poured out my heart to him, and he actually laughed at me! I started to cry and withdrew to my bedroom. I felt alone and betrayed again. I remember wishing I had sisters instead of brothers. Sisters would never have treated me this way, would never have teased me or laughed at me as Peter and Todd had done. I agonized for hours over whether I should really bother to tell my parents, especially after the way Peter had reacted. Finally, I bit the bullet.

I gathered my parents together in the living room and sat down on the couch next to them, the couch that we were not allowed to sit on unless it was a special occasion. The room seemed deadly silent and my heart was pounding. They looked to me in anticipation. I couldn't turn back now and I told them everything about Todd. I told them how he had come into my room for years and molested me. I went into great detail on the specifics of what he did, all the while biting my tongue, wanting to say, "How could you not notice what was happening? Couldn't you see how scared I was of Todd? Didn't you notice that I never looked at him or talked to him across the kitchen table? Didn't you think it was strange when I asked for a lock on my bedroom door? Why did you adopt me if you weren't going to love and protect me? What kind of parents are you?" The moment each word left my mouth, I seemed to forget what I'd said, but I felt the dark mass of that secret escape from me all the same. I felt embarrassed and ashamed. My stomach was in knots. They asked me a million questions I would never be able to remember later, and I wished silently that this would all end, that I could go hide in my room and forget that this ever happened.

I don't know what I expected them to do, or how I thought they would react. I think I hoped they'd feel sorry for me and do something, anything to get Todd out of the house so I would never have to see him again. My confession had shocked them. That I could see. Their questions continued for hours, and I cried until my eyes became puffy and my face grew hot and red with tears. I feared they would bring Todd in the room and tell him what I had said. I just wanted them to make everything right and better so we could be a family and I could be a daughter with parents who loved and protected me like everyone else I knew.

My father had Todd arrested immediately. I'll never forget the look on our neighbors' faces when they put my brother into the back of a police car. We were on public display. I could only imagine what everyone thought, as I had been conditioned to make things look forever good on the outside. It mortified me even more when a police officer escorted me to another squad car to take me to the police station for examination and questioning. How could they treat me like this? After all, Todd had committed the crime, not me. I was the victim, yet they endlessly questioned and scrutinized me on things I didn't want to think about, let alone talk about, until the whole horrible story fell from my lips in a string of words.

I came home later that afternoon and nobody talked about it. It was as if nothing had happened. The family secrets blossomed. My mother never really believed that it had happened at all. She told me on several occasions that I had exaggerated. She refused to believe that her firstborn son was a child molester. Despite the fact that Todd was constantly in trouble and constantly caused problems, she refused to acknowledge that he abused me for years. To this day, we don't talk about it. I hated her for that, and I tried to convince myself that the guilt she must have felt prevented her from acknowledging the unthinkable. She was simply unable, knowing the truth deep down, to do anything to make things right. I started to pray to a God that I really didn't believe in to bring me my birth mother, because this one wasn't working out too well. I also prayed that God would bring me my entire birth family. This one had problems I could no longer deal with.

Todd ended up in jail and our family began attending weekly family therapy sessions while he lived away from home. I detested having to sit in the same room with him. He still terrified me, and it concerned me that he would eventually come back home and hurt me again.

Six months later, my worst fear came true. My parents allowed Todd to come back home. I couldn't believe they allowed him to return after what he'd done to me for so many years. Since my mother never accepted the fact that he'd abused me at all, it's safe to assume it never crossed her mind that it might happen again. But that's exactly what happened. He molested me again.

I couldn't say anything about the abuse this time. Todd had acquired a gun when he lived away from home, and one of the conditions of his return was that my father confiscate it and hide it from him. I'd overheard Todd telling my father he knew where the gun was hidden. I thought back to how threatened I felt by him and I knew he wouldn't allow me a second run to my parents. At this time, I made a conscious decision to run away, whether I thought I'd ever actually do it or not. I knew wholeheartedly that I didn't want to be in this family anymore. I felt alone, vulnerable, afraid, and unprotected. My parents knew what Todd had done to me, and yet they'd let him back into the house so my horror could start all over again. If something like this had ever happened to Todd, I knew they would have fiercely protected him as they had always done, and I felt that they didn't care one way or the other about what happened to me.

My life began to change after Todd's return. At the ripe old age of fifteen, I discontinued my acting career, became sexually active, and began to drink alcohol. I drank heavily from the first time I turned a glass to my lips. I had a lot of demons to run away from, and for some reason, when I drank alcohol those fears went away. In addition to my bingeing and stealing, I began to sneak downstairs at night to steal alcohol from my father's liquor cabinet. I would drink his vodka and fill the bottle back up with water. At times I could be spotted standing in front of 7-Eleven, waiting for someone who would buy me beer, preferably a cheap generic brand. During the weekends my friends started to bring vodka into my room through the sliding glass door while everyone else slept, or I would sneak out the sliding glass door of my bedroom that led to the street. I would stay out all night and drink, then sneak back in before daylight, pass out until noon, then start the process over again the next night.

When I baby-sat at other people's homes, I'd have my friends come over and bring alcohol with them. Otherwise, I told them not to come. As far as I was concerned, if they didn't have alcohol for me, they had nothing to offer and I wanted nothing to do with them. My friendships became shallower and shallower, everything based solely on what they could bring me or do for me.

My mother had always told me that men only thought of women as a piece of meat, and not to trust them. I followed her teachings and, behind her back, began to hang out with boys who could care less whether or not I had a mind. I was so starved for attention and thought so little of myself that if someone paid any attention to me at all, I'd do whatever they wanted. Over the years, my self-esteem had plummeted. I felt unlovable and fat, and thought I should take whatever I could get because I didn't think I deserved anything better.

My first sexual partner was Manny, who lived upstairs from one of my friends. He didn't give a damn about me. If he saw me on the street, he would cruelly taunt me and call me names. He said horrible things that left me feeling worthless. Then, that evening, he'd call me and we would talk like nothing happened and make plans for later that night. I even took him to the prom because I wanted everyone to see me with such a handsome guy. I felt like no one would believe I could date someone so good-looking. The relationship itself was horribly abusive, and yet I clung to it as if I deserved it. To me, any attention beat no attention. I drowned out all the uncomfortable feelings with alcohol, and numbed myself with bingeing and stealing. He called me fat and ugly and I believed him, even though I still wasn't ever more than ten pounds overweight. Though my looks had made me a lot of money in Hollywood, I believed him all the same, just as I'd believed my mother when she felt I was fat.

Manny's handsome features drew me to him. His Italian heritage made him tall and dark with deep green eyes. He loved his car more than he could possibly care for any human being. Though he was twenty-one, he would hang out with us at my friend's apartment where we would all drink. He was the oldest one who hung out there, and he would purchase the alcohol for us and we'd get drunk. I never realized the insanity of it all. My concerns centered only around me, and what I could do to try and make myself feel decent and human. I didn't once think of the ramifications if my parents ever found out how old he was and that I was sexually involved with him. I was only fifteen, but the possibility of my parents arresting him for statutory rape never crossed my mind.

Todd finally moved out for good after I turned sixteen. Thank God! After all those years of fear and humiliation, the molestation finally stopped. It amazes me what fear can do to you, and what can happen when the source of that fear is removed. Amazingly, within a year of his departure, I grew from a petite, flat-chested, four feet eleven to a well-developed five feet seven inches tall. I finally began to menstruate and develop into a young woman. It was as if my paralyzing fear had stunted my bodily growth. It was as if I was afraid to look like a woman, as if by some miracle, if I continued to look like a little girl, Todd would eventually leave me alone. My family, friends, and even I myself had assumed that I was naturally a flat-chested, petite young lady. How could we know otherwise? Not knowing what my birth family looked like, I had no accurate frame of reference in which to compare body types. Little did we know that underneath I really had the genes of a well-developed, hourglass-shaped young lady. Surprisingly and joyfully, I ended up being taller and shapelier than most of my girlfriends. No more "short people got no reason" jokes on my account!

In Todd's absence, Peter and I both became better thieves; he specialized in stealing money, I stuck with stealing food. The thievery caused both of us problems, of course. Whenever something turned up missing, we would both get blamed for it unless one of us fessed up to the crime. If my mother found twenty dollars gone from her purse, she would ground both of us because she knew one of us had perpetrated the act though she could never prove it. And while I admit to stealing food, it wasn't I who had stolen the money, but I was punished just the same.

My mother's punishment and control over me only worsened as the years passed. She became more and more obsessed with my body and weight, and continued to do everything she could to get me the nineteen-inch waist she thought I needed to survive in the world. She started to require that I swim twenty laps a day in the pool in our front yard, the same pool Todd had tried to drown me in only a few years before. Since that time, I'd developed a phobia about pools, even bathtubs. I felt claustrophobic and trapped there. Even though Todd was gone, I was still terrified of him, as if he would suddenly appear in the pool for a repeat performance. I'd also seen "Jaws" one too many times, and believed the great white shark from the movie would somehow swim through the pipes and up through the drain of the pool or bathtub and attack me. So, as I swam laps, my mind filled with terror. I remember the way my heart thumped in my chest as if it might explode, not only because I was swimming as fast as I could to get it over with, but also from fear that I wouldn't make it out of the pool alive.

I was also still afraid of the dark, despite the fact that I was a teenager. Every night as I took the trash out into the dark I felt followed, as if I teetered precariously on the verge of a chase. I had to make my way down a long, dark walkway to get to the trash cans, and I remember how I would frantically run back into the house and slam the door behind me as my heart beat out of my chest. I also couldn't sleep unless I faced the doorway. Even though Todd had left, the thought that he would somehow return to hurt me again frightened me, haunting me in my dreams. There, he could penetrate all doors, come through any lock or window. He permeated my nightmares.

I couldn't tell my mother about my fears because, after all, she would not acknowledge the horrors that Todd had perpetrated on me and everyone else in the family. Neither could I tell my friends about my fear of swimming pools. I was sixteen years old and afraid of swimming pools, bathtubs, and the dark. If I told anyone, they would surely laugh me out of the neighborhood. My mother would definitely think I was foolish, and even crazy to have such concerns as a teenager. So time wore on, and I swam lap after lap as panic drove me every stroke of the way. With every breath, I thought of running away and being free.

I kept my boyfriend, for lack of a better word, a secret from my mother for about a year and a half. Now that I was menstruating, I passed a note in class to a friend and asked her about birth control methods. When I got home, I threw the note into my trash. I never realized that my mother went through my wastebasket to keep an eye on me. She read the note and confronted me about it. I admitted to my sexual activity, lied about how old Manny was, and told her there was nothing she could do about it. She became stricter with me, and in turn, I became more rebellious. She restricted my phone calls to fifteen minutes. When she was out I would stay on the phone much longer, until she came home one day irate that she got a busy signal for more than fifteen minutes. I then learned that she frequently called in to check up on me. If she called and got a busy signal, she would punish me when she got home.

As far as birthdays go, I would have to say that my seventeenth birthday was by far the worst I had ever experienced. On that day, not only did I miss my birth mother, I also lost two of my favorite companions. My aunt Mona died of lung cancer and my dog Sharka was put to sleep after a bout with Fanconi's syndrome, a disease that affects the kidneys. I knew that Mona was dying, as I had visited her in the hospital countless times. I remember going to school the morning of my birthday knowing I would visit her later that afternoon.

But during that school day, Mona died in her sleep and my mother put Sharka to sleep without telling me. I remember coming home from school looking for Sharka, and finding my brother Peter digging a grave in the backyard in preparation for his burial. Words cannot describe how furious I was with my mother for not telling me she was going to put him to sleep that day. I remember crying hysterically, one because my precious aunt Mona was gone, two because my buddy Sharka was put to sleep behind my back, and three because once again I felt that my mother had stabbed me in the back.

I can vividly recall Mona's funeral and how I was afraid to cry, lest I never stop. I missed her so terribly and I cried constantly in secret, but for some reason I was afraid to let my feelings show in public. To make matters worse, I remember my mother telling me that she was ashamed of me for not crying at Mona's funeral. Little did she know how horribly sad I truly was and how I simply did not feel safe enough to cry in front of her. After all, we did not have the kind of relationship where I felt I could go to her, so there was no reason for me to tell her how I was really feeling.

Not long after Mona and Sharka died, Peter introduced me to marijuana. I loved it, maybe more than alcohol. I began to smoke as frequently as possible. When my parents would leave town, I'd throw huge parties at the house with kegs of beer and live disc jockeys. The house would get trashed and the next day

I'd be frantically cleaning the house, taking broken picture frames to the repair shop.

It amazes me that worse things than property damage never occurred. My immaturity at the parties led to irresponsibility. I would often pass out on the couch while the party continued. If I managed to stay conscious, I poured drinks for everyone else and made sure theirs were as strong as mine so I wouldn't be the only one making a fool of myself. My parents never found out. How, I'll never know because the neighbors certainly knew. If my mother and father ever figured it out, they never confronted me about it.

I began to live a secret life. Now I only brought home the friends I knew they would approve of. I kept my drinking and smoking friends, the ones who behaved just as I did, away from home. I continued to get good grades in school, despite having to study twice as hard to remember what I'd read because of all the marijuana I was smoking, and in June in 1985 I graduated from high school. My father came to the ceremony without my mother. In fact, I told my mother not to come. I'd spent many years working hard, hoping it would make her love me, but she was not able to meet my insatiable needs. Now I really didn't care what she thought of me, and the elation that in a few months I would leave for college and be out of the house for good replaced my old fears of being sent away.

I met Reza, my first real boyfriend, soon after high school graduation. He managed the movie theater where I had a summer job. He promoted me to the box office the second day I worked there, an unheard-of managerial move, because he had a crush on me. Of course, I fell instantly in love with him because he paid attention to me. He was the first man I ever loved, or at least the first I ever thought I loved. I had such an unhealthy idea of what love really meant.

Reza, who was twenty-three, treated me very well. He did all the things I thought a decent boyfriend should do—he bought me pot and alcohol whenever I wanted it. He loved me, a sort of desperate love that motivated him to do whatever I wanted. For the first time in my life, I had control over the situation. Reza was so different from Manny, more arduous rather than cruel. It seemed like such an improvement that I thought it must be the true love I had heard talked about so often.

Even though I knew I would miss Reza, I desperately wanted to go away to college. I had to get away from my family. Not surprisingly, my mother did not want me to go away to college. Her preference was for me to stay at home and go to a local college. I applied to both California State University Northridge (CSUN) and the University of California at Santa Barbara (UCSB). I got accepted at both, but my mother insisted I attend CSUN because of the proximity to home. Despite her wishes and implied threats of cutting me off financially, I decided to go to UCSB and get a bachelor's degree in psychology. My father approved, maybe thinking that moving away from home would benefit me, so off I went in September of 1985. Reza stayed behind.

Going away to college was like a dream come true. I had yearned to get away from home, away from the memories of Todd and his leering eyes and the controlling hands of my mother. I had broken free, and the world was my oyster. I wanted to start anew and forget all about the past.

The week I left for college, my parents separated and my mother announced that she had been diagnosed with emphysema. Their separation was a long time coming, and I was relieved when my father finally left. I suppose my parents had some strange idea that it was best to stay together until all of us children had grown up and moved away from home. I didn't agree. I saw how miserable my parents were, how they put up with each other. My parents gave each other the silent treatment more often than they talked together. My mother blamed me for the separation, stating that if it wasn't for me and my behavior, they would have gotten along better. I believed it was my fault for a long time.

My mother now lived alone in that huge house in Beverly Hills, miserable in her own loneliness, while I was away at school refusing to maintain any sort of relationship with her. I didn't want any communication with my father either or any reminders of earlier times. But if I was forced to talk to either one of them, my father was my first choice. My father began to see how unhappy I was and suggested that I go into therapy. I temporarily went to see a counselor just to appease him, but I was not going to let anybody into my life. Obviously, I didn't get any positive results because I refused to deal with the underlying issues. At the time I thought I was doing fine—now that I was away from home. I didn't need anybody. Nobody needed to know my problems. Ironically, after feeling fat my entire life when in reality I was only slightly overweight, I now began to gain weight with a vengeance. I concocted my famous "marijuana and trail mix" diet to combat the weight gain. I ran three miles every night and only ate trail mix and smoked pot. Believe it or not, it worked. But only temporarily.

The problems I had with self-esteem continued. It seemed no matter how smart I was told I was or how well I performed in school, I could never move past my own belief that I was basically worthless and deserved only second-rate attention from men. Reza and I attempted to maintain a long-distance relationship, which basically consisted of ten phone calls a day. He continued to treat me extremely well, so I thought. The only problem was, I was no longer physically attracted to him. In fact, I don't think I ever was. I just equated attention with love. When he bought me booze or marijuana, I thought that meant he loved me. Even knowing that we weren't going anywhere, I thought I should hold on to whatever had been offered me in case nothing better ever came along.

I told myself I loved him. I didn't realize at the time how incapable of that emotion I was. Emotionally, I couldn't trust anyone at all. I didn't understand that because of my adoption, and because of what I had been through in life, it was very hard for me to let people in.

Despite Reza's constant phone calls, I felt hopelessly lonely in life. Though I had friends and enjoyed school, I still didn't feel like I fit in. I made good grades and enjoyed my study of psychology, but I retained little of what I learned. I spent too much time at parties and on the phone with Reza. I didn't really participate in college life. I drove home every weekend to see Reza, except for the one or two weekends when he actually trekked up the coast to see me. As long as he paid attention to me, I couldn't care less how far I had to drive.

My first two years of college seemed very surreal, and reality almost intangible, probably from the perpetual marijuana high I subjected myself to. Even a pregnancy scare barely jarred my irresponsible behavior. The only emotion I could muster was disgust at painting myself into such a corner when I knew I was too young to have children. As soon as I realized I wasn't really pregnant, life continued as usual.

During the summer before my junior year of college, I returned to Los Angeles and transferred to CSUN, partly because they had an excellent psychology program, but mostly because the closer proximity to Reza attracted me. Ironically, I moved back in with my mother in the house where I had grown up. She offered me free rent as long as I went to school full time, and out of some sort of ingrained loyalty, or maybe guilt, I thought I would do a good deed and keep her company. My parents were divorced by now and I felt sorry for her, perhaps still believing that I was somehow to blame, and thought I could try to be the good daughter again. I think that somehow I thought I could make her express her love for me.

In October of 1987, a few days before my twentieth birthday, I broke off my relationship with Reza. We'd stayed together nearly two and a half years, most of that time spent apart. It seems somewhat ironic that I drove an hour and a half to see him every weekend for two years, but had no desire to see him once I was only minutes up the freeway. This later became a pattern of mine—love them from afar, leave them when they are near.

My sense of loyalty to my mother eventually betrayed me. I didn't like her, and she didn't like me. It felt awful to live there as the rift between us widened. She still wouldn't allow me to sit on her gorgeous couch in the living room, though I often did it just to spite her. A lifetime had passed, but nothing had changed. I had to ask permission to use the washer or dryer. When I used the kitchen, I had to leave everything spotless. If she found a single crumb, she would interrupt my studying and insist I clean it up immediately. I guess it was my own fault. What was I thinking by moving back in with her? Even though I was miserable, I stayed there for my entire junior year.

During my senior year, now living with a girlfriend in Chatsworth, just minutes from CSUN, I partied nightly. I threw myself a party for my twenty-first birthday in the recreation room of our apartment complex. I got so drunk that the only thing I remember from the party is being thrown into the pool. This scenario sums up the bulk of my behavior at this time in my life.

My father remarried a woman named Kimberly, and I became truly fond of my new stepmother. Soon after their wedding, I graduated from CSUN in May of 1989. Prior to the ceremony, my mother, who had not come to my high school graduation at my request, told me she wouldn't come to this graduation if Kimberly came. I should have told her how ridiculous her ultimatum made her appear, that she had no right to ask that of me. Instead, I gave in to her demands, and Kimberly stayed away so my mother would come. Deep down, I still had an insatiable desire, however pathetic, to impress my mother with my goodness, so I would never be abandoned again. I never forgave myself for allowing my mother to manipulate me that way, but my behavior was typical of the way I'd acted all my life.

I'd finished my bachelor's degree in psychology in four years, something very few of my friends had managed to do. In spite of it all, I had absolutely nowhere to go. I told myself I would never set foot on a campus again, that school was not for me anymore. Now, I could only face life. I went from job to meaningless job and attempted to get back into acting. I couldn't find a job I liked, and I hooked up with several talent agents who had no intention of sending me on auditions. They sent me to certain photographers to shoot my portfolio and got a kickback for the referral, but that's all they ever did. I did a few small plays and took some acting classes but never seemed to get anywhere—probably because of all the time and energy I spent being drunk and high instead of going to auditions.

I moved into an apartment with two other roommates, and my substance abuse escalated. When I turned twenty-two in October of 1989, people began to tell me they thought I might have a problem with drugs and alcohol. I had also put on thirty pounds because I couldn't stop bingeing on candy. When I became disgusted with my body I went on another diet and lost the thirty pounds, but put it back on with interest. I decided I needed to live on my own because that way I could eat and drink in secret. I often found myself sick with the flu or some other bug, and I thought things would be much better if everyone would just leave me alone.

I found a cute studio apartment in West Los Angeles. I could eat, drink, and smoke pot whenever I wanted and nobody would know. I continued to take acting classes and started to work as a receptionist for a large law firm. I did a horrible job. I showed up late every day, still tired from having passed out the night before. My supervisor at the firm asked me repeatedly if I really wanted to work there, because my behavior indicated that I didn't. I hated that job. I hated answering phones and I hated all the people. In general, I just hated everything. I was twenty-two years old with a bachelor's degree in psychology that went unused, and I felt like I had nowhere to go.

Chapter 3

Recovery

The time had come to make a change in my life. I was truly reaching what I now know to be a bottom. Everyone else could see it but me. It became clear to me that all the years of therapy, beginning in college, were not working. Although I liked the attention of the therapists, I could never muster enough honesty to facilitate a healing process. Even in the confines of their offices, with full knowledge of the rules of doctor-patient confidentiality, I could never tell them the truth. I never let any of them in. I didn't want anyone to get too close, lest I be abandoned again. Every time a therapist brought up the topic of my adoption, I maintained a heavy denial about the pain surrounding it. I vehemently claimed that it did not affect my life, though I still secretly yearned for my birth mother, hoping she would find me and bring me happiness. I lied about how I felt and told them and everyone else that I didn't care that I was adopted. I convinced myself that despite all the questions and fantasies, I had no interest in knowing my birth mother. I was confident that my mother did not want to know me, because if she did, she would have found me by then, or she wouldn't have given me up in the first place. I guess you could say I basically refused to let myself think about my birth mother. It was too painful, and at the time, I was simply not ready to deal with it.

With the help of my father's financial assistance, I lost thirty pounds on the Jenny Craig diet. Nothing ever worked so well for me. I looked good and felt great. For a while, I actually enjoyed life. I thought I could obtain the body I had wanted all my life. Slowly but surely, I gained the weight back, and depression set in again. For years, my therapists and friends told me that I might have a problem with food. I didn't realize that stealing food and bingeing weren't normal, even though I had always gone to great lengths to hide my behavior. I didn't want to believe I had a problem.

I could only manage a few days of sane eating before I broke down again and binged. I abstained and binged in a repetitive pattern and beat myself up every time I gave in to temptation. I alternated between being remotely pleased when I could manage to eat normally, and scolding and hating myself when I would slip. The same pattern existed with alcohol and marijuana. I would go a few days without them and then have to do something to ease my discomfort. I knew I needed help so I read book after book on eating disorders, talked to people who had experience with addictions, and prayed to a God I wasn't sure existed to remove the obsession. Little by little, I began to comprehend the things they said and the books I read—that I had a serious addiction that should be treated as a disease.

On June 24, 1990, my day started as usual. I woke up around noon, grabbed a bag of cookies and a joint, and went up to the roof to lie out and get a suntan. I binged all afternoon and listened to rock music on the radio. Suddenly, out of the blue, I started to cry, got down on my knees and asked God to help me change my life. I realized how miserable I'd become. I saw with amazing clarity the way I'd wasted my life, the way I lived without purpose, killing myself bit by bit, day by day. I tried to smoke some pot to calm myself down, but found to my horror that I couldn't get high. I smoked and smoked and smoked, and nothing happened. It scared me to death. I switched to drinking, watched a movie, and passed out in front of the television.

I woke up a few hours later disoriented, and by some miracle, I recognized that I truly had a problem. For the first time in my life, I admitted to myself that I had an eating disorder and a problem with alcohol and marijuana. The thought occurred to me that just maybe my depression, inability to hold a job, and relationship difficulties might somehow be rooted in my substance abuse. In hindsight, I suppose you could say I had a spiritual experience. I "saw the light." I saw the lack of direction in my life and that the reason I wanted to be alone all the time, the reason I felt so afraid, was because I had a sickness within me. I saw, finally, my addiction to food, as well as my addictions to alcohol and marijuana.

I had some pot out on the coffee table and it scared me that I might smoke it. For the first time, I conceived that once I started, I couldn't stop. I didn't know what to do and settled on a call to my father begging him to come over. I flushed the pot and all the alcohol down the toilet, and sat on my hands until he got there.

My father came over, held me, and let me cry on his shoulder as I continued to babble about everything I'd been hiding from him for years. I must have sounded hysterical to him as I rambled nonsensically about my fears and apprehensions. I can't remember much of what he said, other than his repeated reassurance that I'd be all right. He asked me if I'd flushed the drugs down the toilet, and I could honestly say that I had. An inner excitement brewed in me. I could sense the potential for change. For hours, I ranted and raved to him, telling him all the horrible things I had done. How I was a thief and a liar and a cheat. Three hours later, my father put me to bed, waited for me to fall asleep, and went home.

I awoke the next morning and realized a miracle had happened. It was June 25, 1990, and I was clean and sober. The obsession was lifted, something years of therapy and endless reading could not accomplish. I had prayed to God to take me out of my misery, and now I felt truly alive, something I hadn't felt in years. I had a moment of clarity when a switch went on inside my head and I realized I no longer had to smoke or drink alcohol, at least not that day. I cried a lot over the next few days, not really knowing why, but I just let myself feel whatever emotions came up. On June 29, I abstained from bingeing, and felt strongly that it might be the last time I'd have to do that behavior as well. I no longer binged, stole food, or ate sugar, and it felt great.

Once I got through the crying stage and began to get myself together, I started taking acting classes with a vengeance. I rehearsed my scenes and impressed my coaches. They saw a change in me that they couldn't explain, but I knew exactly what it was. My head was free and clear to focus on the craft. Shortly after I began acting classes, I got the lead role in an original musical. In short, I felt elated. It seemed my life was beginning to turn around.

As a result of abstaining from the substances that I came to believe were killing me, I suddenly had too much time on my hands. So what was I to do? Pick up a new obsession. While working on the musical, I met Mark DeFazio. About a month had passed since I'd become clean, sober, and abstinent from bingeing. My weight had dropped substantially, the dark circles under my eyes were dissipating, and I was starting to feel attractive for the first time in my life. Needless to say, I fell in love with the wrong man at first sight.

I had quit my job at the law firm and he was unemployed, so we had lots of time to spend together.

He also had a lead role in the musical, and we had lots
of fun rehearsing and studying lines. I felt like someone
finally understood me. I'd found a man who listened to
me and paid attention to me, and as my old patterns
dictated, I became obsessed.

In due time, Mark showed his true colors. He was a
big guy, a bulimic, and often became violent and angry,
not unlike my brother Todd. He'd lost his last job after
he hit his boss. He had a bad temper, and most of my
friends, even my father, warned me to be wary of
him. Of course, I didn't listen. How could there be
something wrong with the man I loved?

At Christmastime in 1990, six months clean, sober,
and abstinent, I went to a Christmas caroling party with
Mark and my girlfriend Stephanie, who was visiting
from out of town and staying at my apartment. Mark
and I ended up in a fight and argued the whole
evening. It started on the way to the party and lasted
all night long. Afterwards, Stephanie, Mark, and I all
returned to my place. I was furious with him. I'd finally
had it with his hair-trigger temper and unending rage,
which he often directed at me. I broke up with him on
the spot. Not surprisingly, he drove off in a fit of rage.
Upset yet relieved that he was gone, I got ready for bed.

Twenty minutes later, the phone rang. It was Mark,
hysterical, angry, and begging to come over and work
things out. He claimed undying love for me, said that
he needed me, that he would change his ways and
never let it happen again. I could tell something inside
him had snapped, and for the first time, the thought of

what he might do truly scared me. After he hung up, I
called our mutual friend Sam and asked him to come
over quickly, all the while thanking God that Stephanie
was with me. Unfortunately, Sam lived about twenty
minutes away, and before he could arrive, Mark was
pounding on my front door. It got louder and louder
with each passing second. He had somehow managed
to bypass the security gate in front of my building.
My heart almost jumped out of my throat every time
he beat on that door. Surely he would attack me the
moment he broke through it. I closed my eyes and
hoped against everything that the door would hold for
just a moment more so Sam could arrive and save me.
Only God knows why I didn't think to call 911.

Suddenly the door broke free of one of the hinges.
Only a ninety-nine-cent security chain that I'd installed
myself less than a week earlier kept the door in place.
Stephanie and I screamed. That little chain couldn't
possibly compete against Mark's brute strength and
size. In a matter of a few short, hysterical breaths, the
only barrier that separated us from the maniac he'd
become would fall away. Thankfully, Sam arrived
seconds before Mark managed to completely dismantle
the door. He made swift progress and calmed Mark
down before he could fly into hysteria again. The four
of us attempted to discuss what had happened like civil
adults. I was very unforgiving and I gave him back
a promise ring he had given me. I told him in no
uncertain terms to go away and never come back.

The next few days, Mark called me obsessively, often

five times a day or more to tell me he loved me and to apologize for his behavior. He promised to pay me for the damages to my door and asked if there was anything he could do to make it up to me. I convinced myself that we had shared a deep love, and he was obviously having a hard time surviving the end of our relationship. On one hand, it terrified me to see his true self; I thought he would someday hurt me if I gave him the chance to do it again. On the other hand, I could only see a man who paid a lot of attention to me, who told me he loved me and that I meant the world to him. He told me he would change and I desperately wanted to believe him. I wanted a boyfriend more than I wanted to be alone. To the chagrin of my father and after much pleading by Mark, my desperation led me back to him, and we got back together only three weeks later.

In June of 1991, my father and I went to see Mark perform in a production of "My Fair Lady." It was closing night, and it was Father's Day. Mark had requested that I bring my father to see the performance, and I couldn't understand why, since my father had often shown an overt dislike for Mark and the way he treated me. Soon Mark's intentions became all too clear.

At curtain call, the music stopped, and the leading man came to the front of the stage to address the audience. He said it was a special day for a member of the cast, and he needed a certain young lady in the sixth row to come up onto the stage to help the cast member out. I began to shake. I was petrified. I knew he was referring to me, and I sure as hell didn't want to get up onto the stage, actress or no actress. My father, partly out of frustration at the blatant disregard I had shown toward his warnings about Mark, angrily told me that I'd better get up there, and I begrudgingly made my way to the stage.

About fifteen hundred people sat in the audience. I could feel every single set of eyes upon me. I knew what was going to happen, and I knew that it was wrong. It felt like everything happened in slow motion, and background sounds became buried in the wind that rushed loudly into my ears. When I got onto the stage, Mark dropped to one knee and sang our favorite love song to me. I began to look around nervously, unwilling to hold his gaze. I could only think of how I wanted to click my heels together so I could instantly get home, away from this uncomfortable experience, this dread in the pit of my stomach. At that same moment, he completed the song and asked me to marry him.

I wanted to say no, to yell from the rooftops, to tell him I deserved better, that I needed more. The word caught in my throat. It seemed an eternity before I answered. I knew that I didn't want to marry this moody, angry man, and that deep down, I didn't love him. I looked out over the audience where people now stood up, clapping and cheering. Some even cried, and

I was afraid. I knew my father disapproved of him, but in the end that didn't matter. Mark paid attention to me, and I needed that more than the approval of my father. I turned to him and said yes.

The next day, I moved in with Mark. Looking back, I didn't want to, but things had begun to happen of their own accord. In a single day, my whole life changed. I moved from my sweet little studio apartment in West Los Angeles that I so truly loved, to a run-down dive in Highland Park, a city with a reputation for gang activity. Even though I had been able to change my life in many ways as far as drinking and using is concerned, I was not able to see the path of destruction I was headed down when it came to relationships. Mark and I made our wedding plans, and my friends humored me by pretending to go along with it, when everyone but me knew what a huge mistake I was about to make.

My father even sat me down and made a serious attempt to convince me not to marry Mark, but I didn't want to hear anything about it. In truth, I tried to forget the fact that Mark took five or six medications for anxiety and depression, that he was a bulimic who was vomiting daily, and that he couldn't hold down a job. My father had recognized in Mark a look that said he wasn't quite right, and he urged me to reconsider. His belief was that I could do much, much better.

In February of 1992, about eight months after Mark and I moved in together, I got a job as the bookkeeper of a retirement home in Glendale. Since he remained unemployed, he became the happy homemaker. He had dinner on the table for me when I came home at night, and I thought that was love. The fact that he put holes in the walls after dinner changed that belief. He was still subject to random acts of violence, and I never knew what would set him off.

While he often acted out by destroying property and punching or kicking holes in the walls, he never hit me, and this became the reassurance I needed that things would end up all right. Besides, he paid attention to me, and my father already had five thousand dollars invested in our wedding. Despite the warnings of almost everyone in my life, I decided I would stay with him as long as he never hurt me. After all, he never really verbally abused me too badly, though he abused himself and was in a rage most of the time. I told myself if he ever hit me, that would end it.

We married in April of 1992. I remember walking down the aisle, my hand in the nook of my father's arm as I sobbed uncontrollably. Apparently, a part of me knew I was making the biggest mistake of my life, even though I refused to accept it. Needless to say, I didn't invite Todd to the wedding, and my mother and Peter refused to come. Every shred of my soul, every fiber of my being, told me I shouldn't go through with it, and I screamed on the inside as I tried to figure out some way, any way, to get out of it, but I couldn't bring myself to take the action. I stood there in front of the minister, in front of my family and friends, in front of God, and swore to be with Mark forever.

Immediately following the ceremony, Mark got into a

fight with the photographer and fired him, so we didn't have any formal photographs of the wedding. The pictures that my friends and family took showed my disgust and embarrassment on the day that was supposed to be the happiest of my life. At the reception, Mark argued with his parents and made a few scenes. In general, I didn't particularly enjoy myself. We went to the hotel, the place where our honeymoon should have commenced, and he ended up on the phone with his mother, begging her to forgive him for his behavior at the wedding and reception. It horrified me to see what my marriage had already turned out to be—a colossal mess, what our rocky relationship had always been since the beginning.

The marriage was awful from the start. I became increasingly afraid of him and lived in fear again, just as I had when I lived under the same roof with my brother Todd. I suffered many sleepless nights and went to work tired, grateful I had a job at the retirement home. Two months following the wedding, and after several years of unemployment, Mark finally managed to find work with the gas company. However, he was chronically miserable and complained about his job all the time. I finally knew it would only be a matter of time before he lost that job, just like all the others, and I would have to support him again.

A month after he started the job, he called me at work, something he had done often and compulsively. He was in a rage again, and asked me if I would go to court as moral support for him while he testified against his previous employer, whom he had struck. Although by this time I'd grown used to his antics, his endless complaints, angry outbursts, and unreasonable demands, something finally woke me up. I decided I didn't want to continue another day with him. In that moment I made the decision to leave my marriage. I told Mark I didn't support his behavior and would never go to court with him. He became hysterical and hung up on me.

I immediately called my closest ally against Mark—my father. He happily agreed to help me move out and away from my husband. The next day, I found an apartment in Glendale after only three hours of looking. Frankly, I didn't care where I lived or what shape the place was in, as long as I lived away from Mark. The fact that I found a nice place in such a short time told me that fate had determined I leave him after only three months of marriage. At that point, I knew I never should have married him in the first place.

My father and I planned the move for the following Tuesday. Mark would be at work and I could take the day off. My father and I moved everything in a matter of only a few hours, and I got an unlisted telephone number so Mark couldn't harass me. My new apartment was small but charming, and I finally felt safe without any fear that Mark would find out where I lived. My certainty about this wavered only briefly that evening when I got a call from the telephone company. They said an irate man by the name of Mark DeFazio had called and claimed to be my husband. He demanded to know my phone number and where I lived. When I arranged for my phone, I told them not to give the information out under any circumstances, and felt grateful for their stringent rules and regulations. They refused to tell him anything.

It was July of 1992 and I was free. I ended up filing a summary dissolution, the equivalent of a divorce that can be granted if the marriage lasts under five years, no property is owned, and no children are produced. It ran me about five hundred dollars, which I had to pay myself, since Mark refused to participate financially in the divorce. I wanted nothing more to do with him, so the money was no object.

During my divorce process, at the age of twenty-four, I had every intention of leaving the past behind me. Despite my best efforts to the contrary, thoughts of my birth mother started to haunt me again. For over two years at this point, I had successfully squelched my feelings about wanting to know who and where she was. I didn't know what else to do but to start nurturing my spirituality and my relationship with God.

I entered therapy again, this time opening up and telling the truth. I began to let down my walls and I finally stopped pretending I wasn't affected by being adopted. I was finally able to admit that I did care, I was curious, and that it did cause me a lot of pain not knowing my roots. I worked with my counselor instead of against her. I admitted to my faults, my addictions, my relationship difficulties, and the fact that I was very angry with my adoptive mother. I admitted that all my problems were perhaps related to my deep-seated issue —that I was in a lot of pain surrounding the loss of my birth mother and the fact that I was adopted into an abusive home.

By this time I'd stayed clean, sober, and abstinent from bingeing for two years and it was time to clear away the wreckage of my childhood. I made amends to my mother for telling her that I would find my birth mother and leave her. I made amends for stealing her food and for defying her. I made amends for throwing wild parties in her house. I made amends to my brothers for stealing food from them. I made amends to my father for stealing his alcohol and only calling him when I wanted money in college. I made financial amends to my father for telling him that my college textbooks cost more than they actually did. I made financial amends to stores and institutions that I had stolen from. Store managers were amazed that someone would come back years later with a check in hand and a sincere apology. When I made financial amends to the neighborhood grocery store that I used to frequent, the manager remembered me. He told me he had been waiting for me. Needless to say, I never stole from people or institutions again. In fact, I started to become rigorously honest about my life. I showed up for work on time, did a good job, and paid my bills on time. When a cashier accidentally gave me too much change, I would promptly go back to the store and return it, or when the waiter forgot to charge me for something I ordered, I would remind him of it. These were things I wouldn't dream of doing earlier. Being clean and sober and leading an honest life forced me to behave this way.

As part of recovery, I discovered that not only was I furious with my mother for treating me harshly and not believing that Todd had molested me, but my anger toward her was interfering with my life. I attempted to talk to her about how I felt so hurt when she acknowledged the attempted drowning incident by weighing me, but she did not want to discuss it with me. Our conversations inevitably led to her bragging about Todd and how wonderful he was. Knowing how I felt about Todd, she insisted on telling me time and time again what great things he was doing with his life. I knew she continued to think the world of him—despite overwhelming evidence to the contrary— and I had trouble comprehending what she was talking about because the Todd I knew was living with Elizabeth and was verbally and sometimes physically abusive to her. He was supposed to be taking care of her as she suffered from dementia, but instead he stole from her. Finally, I mustered the courage to request that she not mention him in our conversations. I explained as best I could that I wanted to hear about her life, and I didn't care to hear about his. When she wasn't able to honor my request, I cut off further communication with her. Many friends had suggested that I needed some time away from her to work through my childhood issues and my anger toward her.

I also discovered I was furious with my father for not protecting me from my mother or Todd. My father, however, was always willing to listen to me. He admitted that he was an absent father and that he was preoccupied with my brothers' shenanigans. He also apologized for not stepping in when he saw my mother treating me poorly. Thankfully, as a result of our many conversations and amends made to each other, we developed a loving relationship, one in which I was able to tell him I loved him, something I was never able to do before.

In December of 1992, five months into my divorce proceedings, I took up country dancing and was participating up to four nights a week. It was on the dance floor that I met Jeffrey. Jeffrey was a successful computer programmer who was financially stable, something I found attractive. The relationship started out great, but soon after the initial "honeymoon" period wore off, he started to become overly critical of me. He criticized my choices in clothing, jobs, and hairstyles. He even told me that I should lose the ten pounds of excess weight I was carrying. Even though he was a definite improvement in my choice of men, I was bothered by the criticism. I convinced myself that he was a "keeper" because he didn't punch holes in the wall like Mark did. When we danced together, I wanted to be perfect for him because he danced with skill and grace and had aspirations to compete. I wanted to be his partner on and off the dance floor. Unfortunately, I couldn't dance up to snuff for him. Despite the excuse that I didn't practice as much as he did, I just plain couldn't dance at his level. To make matters worse, I tried so hard to impress him that it only resulted in more mistakes. I felt his disappointment in me, and disappointment is one thing I've never been able to handle.

As far as our relationship went, it came down to the fact that he wanted children. I didn't, never had, but I had become willing to have children for him. I think he sensed my desperation and in May of 1993, he broke off the relationship with me just a few weeks after my divorce from Mark was finalized. Obviously, having children just to keep a man is pretty pathetic. When I look back, I see how tragic it would have been to stay with someone like him. That doesn't mean it didn't break my heart when he broke up with me. As usual, I convinced myself he forgot about me within the hour. I, on the other hand, wallowed in misery.

In June of 1993, a month after Jeffrey and I broke up, Elizabeth passed away—a blessing, as it followed years of suffering from dementia. During that time she no longer recognized me.

In January of 1994, I rang in the new year by reverting back to my maiden name, despite pleading from Mark to keep the name DeFazio. But he had moved out of the state, so what was I worried about? I loved my job at the retirement home and planned to stay there forever. I was very pleased with myself because previously I was never able to enjoy any job, or even hold one very long for that matter. I basically ran the place and received their "Employee of the Year" award for 1993.

Despite my success in the workplace, I felt something was missing. What my job lacked was passion and challenge. How ironic that I had trouble keeping jobs, and now I was looking for more challenge in my work. In the blink of an eye I decided to look into graduate school programs. I surprised myself with the decision, because five years earlier I had vowed never to return to school. After careful thought and self-searching examination, I came to the conclusion that I would sell myself short if I stayed at the retirement home. I knew I could do better. I had remained clean, sober, abstinent from bingeing, had escaped a horrible situation with Mark, and just had my heart broken by Jeffrey, so what did I have to lose? I felt unstoppable, like I could accomplish anything I set my mind to.

I decided to become a marriage and family therapist and retire at the age of fifty to go back to acting. My friends always told me that I was a good listener and had a soothing quality about me. I knew I couldn't do much with my bachelor's degree in psychology, so I decided to get my master's. I went to my old alma mater, CSUN, for an orientation meeting on the graduate programs there, which included a master's program in marriage and family therapy. During the orientation, I discovered the field of school psychology.

Prior to the orientation, I knew nothing about the field of school psychology, but I knew I enjoyed working with children and the study of psychology. I found out it involved educational assessments and counseling of students from kindergarten through age twenty-two. I would be working with learning-disabled, emotionally disturbed, mentally retarded, and autistic children. I did a lot of research and found that many more job opportunities existed for school psychologists than for therapists. I took an introductory class in school psychology and became hooked. I promptly decided to get my master's of science degree in counseling with a school psychology credential, with acting still part of the plan after retirement.

I applied to the school psychology master's program at CSUN but didn't get in. Too many students had applied for their program, so I went over to California State University at Los Angeles. I discovered they had an excellent school psychology program as well, and became excited until I found out that the deadline for applications was the following day. But once I set my mind on something, I can't think of anything else, and the thought of having to wait another year seemed like an eternity. I felt strongly that if I didn't do it now, I might never do it at all, so I moved quickly and asked three people to fax me letters of recommendation. I went home and hammered out the mandatory five-page letter of intention. Miraculously, I came in just under the deadline. Shortly thereafter, I jubilantly discovered that the school had accepted me into their three-year, full-time program that admitted only twelve students a year.

I began school in September of 1994, shortly before my twenty-seventh birthday, a time that continued to distress me. But this year I had a distraction—graduate school. At twenty-seven, my life looked good. It consisted of full-time employment at the retirement home, a full class load in the evenings, hours of studying and paper writing, and late nights filled with country dancing, all of which I thoroughly enjoyed.

Even though I thrived on my busy schedule, I began to feel dizzy, fatigued, and off balance—quite a change from my usual boundless energy. I would also become irritable if I didn't eat every three hours, and would fall asleep in class. I went to the doctor and she asked me the infamous question that had been asked of me many times before: What is your family medical history? As I was not able to answer her questions, she ran many tests and discovered that I was dangerously hypoglycemic. As a result, I had to change my diet, eat more frequently, and completely cut out sugar. At this point I began to think about the ramifications of not knowing my medical history. What if I had diabetes in my family? After all, hypoglycemia is often a precursor to diabetes. I had a right to know if I was in danger of developing this debilitating disease. I also started getting migraine headaches and was diagnosed with TMJ, a painful jaw disorder, and wondered if anybody in my family suffered from them as well. I knew I was under stress with my heavy workload and school schedule, but it didn't ease my concern as to what was happening in my body.

I eventually asked the doctor who had diagnosed my hypoglycemia to write a letter to the agency where I was adopted and request family medical records. She stated in her letter that it was a medical necessity that she have knowledge of these records in order to get an accurate picture of my susceptibility to diseases that run in families, namely diabetes, cancer, migraines, etc. Not surprisingly, no response came. So what else could I do but go along with the information I had and take care of myself as best I could.

About two years after I cut off contact with my adoptive mother, I got in touch with her again, as I felt that I had worked through my anger and resentment toward her. Sadly, our relationship did not improve. She was still unable to follow through with an intention or a promise. Since I was a starving student, she told me she would gladly finance a computer I needed for graduate school. Unfortunately I got my hopes up and eagerly shopped for the best computer package available. When I went to her with the results of my research, she decided that she was not able to purchase a computer for me after all. She changed her mind without reason or warning.

In October of 1994, I was on my way to a promising career, and except for a rocky relationship with my mother, I was basically content with the way my life was going. Although my mother decided not to help me out financially, I was pleased that with the help of my job at the retirement home, I was able to put myself through school and have some pocket change to spare for an occasional popcorn and a movie. I was busy studying, mending my relationships, working on myself, and looking forward to my future work with children.

Only my birth mother was missing. Although she was absent from my life, no matter how hard I tried, she was never absent from my thoughts. Ironically, at a party one night I overheard a woman tearfully talk about how she had once put her daughter up for adoption and had finally found her. Just hearing her tell this story made me melancholy that my birth mother had never tried to find me. It was at that moment when I decided I was going to find her.

Once I made this decision, I felt an immediate sense of peace come over me. It was as if a huge weight was lifted from my shoulders. I guess subconsciously I knew that I would eventually come to this place in my life where the next indicated step was to conduct my search for her. But there was no warning. It just hit me. One second I was thinking of her, and the next second I told myself to stop thinking and start acting. Now was the time. It felt like the universe was gently pushing me to do this. Perhaps my higher power thought I was ready now, and not a minute sooner.

Over the next few weeks I had an overwhelming feeling of God's assurance, and I somehow knew I was destined to find the woman who gave me life. I knew with certainty that there was a divine plan laid out for me and that everything would be all right. I planted the idea in my mind that I would find my birth mother when I finished graduate school in June of 1997. That would give me time to investigate search options and it would give me time to mentally prepare for the moment when I would look into the eyes of my beloved birth mother. I told my friends about my plan and they all supported me. After all, they had asked me for years whether I was ever going to look for my real family. I could no longer pretend that the curiosity of my origins wasn't killing me. I would have over two and a half years to prepare. I would be twenty-nine years old. I couldn't wait to see what lay ahead for me. Only time would tell.

Chapter 4

Reunion

It was the evening of Monday, December 5, 1994, only two months after I had made the decision to search for my birth mother. I was sitting quietly at home studying for winter term finals, the first set of finals of my graduate school career. I had the windows drawn, a dim light illuminating my desk where I sat and studied the intricacies of learning disabilities and memorized definitions and terminology. I demanded complete quiet when I studied, so the TV and radio sat silent. You could have heard a pin drop. Only the intermittent sound of light rain on the windows created any noise at all.

Suddenly the phone rang, sounding remarkably loud in my bubble of silence. My friends, ever respectful of my academic aspirations, knew about finals and would never call if they knew I was busy studying. When I answered, the sound of an elderly woman on the other end of the line confounded me even more. The only other elderly woman who ever called me was Elizabeth, but she was long gone now.

"Is your name Kasey Hamner?" she asked, and I immediately assumed it was a saleswoman since I did not recognize her voice.

"Yes," I said, still prepared to hang up if the proposition of a sale arose. I wanted to return to my studying.

"Were you born on October 12th, 1967?"

I paused for a moment and thought about whether or not I should answer. Why would a saleswoman ask me to verify my date of birth?

"Yes . . .," I replied slowly, as a million questions began to dance through my head.

"Did you grow up in Beverly Hills, California?" she asked.

By this time, she'd provoked me into annoyance. Why had she suddenly involved me in some sort of Spanish Inquisition? What could she possibly be selling to necessitate such a barrage of questions, and how on earth did she know so much about me? Maybe I'd won a huge prize, and Ed McMahon lingered outside, ready to knock on my door to hand me an oversized check. It didn't seem like a crank call. In any case, I felt uncomfortable.

"Yes," I said again, ready to hang up the phone if she bombarded me with yet another question.

A long pause ensued and I heard a deep sigh on the other end of the line. I thought she didn't sound energetic enough to work with Ed McMahon, and if this was someone's idea of a sales pitch, it was a horrible one.

"My name is Elaine Geiger," she said.

"So what?" I thought. I was ready to slam the phone down in frustration. I began to open my mouth to say a polite "no thank you" to whatever she was giving away or selling, but before I had the chance, she spoke again and her words stopped me cold.

"I have reason to believe that I'm your birth grandmother."

For a moment, I couldn't speak. In fact, I practically couldn't think straight. Maybe I hadn't heard her right or maybe it was my mind that had fooled me into a believable daydream. Nonetheless, my immediate feeling was, "Oh, my God!" Out of the blue, this unknown woman on the other end of the line, whom I thought of until now as only a saleswoman, had both shocked and amazed me.

"How did you find me?" I asked in disbelief. It was the first question that came to mind, though a thousand others had begun to queue up behind it.

She told me that after twenty-seven years of thinking about me, she simply called directory assistance when she finally found out my name. She said she would love to tell me the rest of the story someday. I immediately thought to myself how grateful I was that I went back to my maiden name in January of that year. Otherwise, I would have been listed under Kasey DeFazio. Another long pause followed. I broke it when I said, "Thank you for finding me." They were only five words, but they meant everything I felt at that moment. It didn't take long before my protective floodgates opened wide and I began to talk.

I told her about my plans to find my birth mother, her daughter, in the summer of 1997, and how I'd never entertained the notion of an extended family. She laughed, a sound as musical to my ears as any I could imagine, and told me many relatives were eagerly waiting to meet me. My thrill and excitement pleased her. All this time, she'd hesitated to contact me, afraid I wouldn't feel happy at being found at all, and here I was, thanking her for taking the time to look.

That first call consisted of a lot of questions and answers, both on her part and mine. It seemed we talked about everything, though it would take years and years to uncover all the stories to be told. It turned out that she lived in Chatsworth, minutes away from the apartment I had kept during my senior year at CSUN. It shocked me to think about the smallness of the world, and the chance that we might have passed by each other on several occasions. In fact, we joked about how we had probably shopped in the same supermarket, how we'd probably even shopped there at the same time and didn't even know it. My mind reeled with the information. Mostly, I asked her about my mother, and why she had given me up. Elaine told me I needed to ask Vanessa myself.

Vanessa. That was my mother's name. I never thought I'd discover the syllables on my own. I thought about the name, and wondered about Vanessa and what kind of person she was. For the first time in my life, I had a name for the woman I had thought about and dreamt about ever since the agency took me away from her immediately after my birth. Remarkably, Vanessa lived within thirty miles of me my entire life!

Of course, I wanted to talk to Vanessa immediately. It upset me when Elaine revealed that she had yet to tell Vanessa she had located me, as Vanessa was against searching for me in the first place. Elaine told me that she and her youngest daughter, my aunt Liz, were the ones who insisted on finding me, with or without Vanessa's permission. When I asked her why Vanessa didn't want to find me, she insisted that I talk to Vanessa directly about it. Elaine assured me that she would let Vanessa know I had been found, but that she was ill with strep throat and probably couldn't call me for a few days. Needless to say, I had trouble accepting this information. I had waited a lifetime to meet her, had made plans to find her, and now I learned that she didn't want to find me. I didn't understand it, but had no other choice than to wait for her to call on her own.

Elaine proceeded to tell me that her husband, my grandfather Nathaniel, passed away seven years earlier. She commented on how sad she was that he didn't get a chance to meet me. She told me my aunt Liz was only fourteen when I was born and was now married to James, twenty years her senior. I had an uncle named Mark, who was in Vietnam when I was born. She told me that on my mother's side I had a half brother named Adam, who was seven years younger than me. He was a college student in northern California. She told me my father's name was Jeffrey, the same name as my ex-boyfriend! What are the odds. Jeffrey had a daughter named Michelle, who was four years older than me, and four sisters, Rebecca, Kari, Anne, and Meredith—my aunts. With each mention of a relative, I could barely contain myself. The names of my newfound family members chimed like music in my ears, like I had never heard those same sounds ever before. They sounded so different from Peter and Todd, Pat and Connie. The knowledge of my birth mother alone amazed me. While I'd often dreamt of her, it never crossed my mind to wonder about any other relatives that might exist. Finally, I knew my last name would have been Sobel.

I stayed on the phone with Elaine for over an hour. We exchanged phone numbers and addresses, and we promised to meet the following weekend—like relatives who did this all the time. I called all my friends to share the news and I tried to return to my studies, but my mind insisted on wandering around fresh new thoughts about the call I'd received. How could I possibly think about finals when I'd just been handed the key to my identity, the one I'd waited for my whole life? As it turned out, I needn't have bothered to try and study anymore that night. I received another phone call less than an hour after Elaine's. This time, the woman on the other end of the line sounded much younger. It was my aunt Liz.

We hit it off immediately. She lived in Monterey, up in northern California, with her husband, James, and their golden retriever, Stu. We shared a lot of common experiences. Liz and I had both been performers as children, and had both gotten married to losers who couldn't hold a job, soon followed by divorce. When we turned to the inevitable discussion of my life, we discovered that Liz and James's favorite movie was the one and only feature film that I was in as a child. We had other coincidental things in common. For instance, we both had a dog named Sandy growing up. In fact, we shared so many things in common that it was almost eerie. As I talked to her on the phone and felt such bonds, even from something as simple as the name of a childhood dog, I experienced for the first time what it felt like to belong, if even just a little, to a family. Liz said she wanted to meet me, and would come down to Elaine's house for our family reunion the following weekend. She said she hadn't been down to L.A. in years, but since it was such a special occasion, she could hardly stay away.

After a couple of hours on the phone, we finally hung up and I took a deep breath. It seemed like I had never taken such a breath, like life had never felt so absolutely precious. That's when all the emotions kicked in. Up to this point, it hadn't exactly sunk in yet that my dream of finding my birth mother was finally coming true, much sooner than I had planned. I felt so many different emotions all at once; then some emotions began to overpower the others. The excitement and joy quickly dissipated, and before long, sadness set in. So much had happened that it shocked my entire system. Was I ready for this? Are you ever ready for something so life-altering as this? How do you know if you are ready? What are the signs? I wasn't sure what the answers were. I actually began to shake and I cried for about three hours. I cried and cried and cried, not knowing why I was crying at all, but I recognized an underlying relief that began to settle. It came from knowing I truly belonged somewhere, to someone's family.

I continued to weep uncontrollably. I didn't know why I'd become consumed with racking sobs, and it confused me. I felt I should be happy. There seemed no reason to be sad. Then it hit me: I was finally truly allowing myself to feel the sorrow of being separated from my mother for nearly three decades. For the first time in my life, I allowed myself to feel all the sadness and anger that I had bottled up for so long. No more talking about it. No more conjecturing what it would be like to meet my birth mother. No more fantasizing about her. Even though I was working hard in therapy by dealing with my feelings and issues of growing up adopted, it didn't prepare me for the fact that suddenly I had another family—complete with aunts, uncles, and cousins—that had been carrying on their lives without me. My emotions swung from rage over not knowing about them until now, to sadness over what I missed out on.

I was embarking on a new phase in my life. Life as I had previously known it had ended, and a new chapter had begun. I would experience no more uncertainty about who I was and where I'd come from. My life's script would begin to rewrite itself. Truth would now replace the plethora of fantasies I'd had growing up. Reality could be painful, I knew, but I hoped I was ready. All I could do now was wait for a call from Vanessa, my long-lost but never forgotten mother.

The next day, I somehow made it in to work. It's amazing I actually made it in at all. I felt like a changed woman, like someone given a second chance at life. I couldn't concentrate on my duties, and couldn't wait for my boss to come in so I could tell her the news. She knew of my plans to search for my birth mother in the coming years, and the thought of telling someone who'd followed my eager planning excited me. I waited at my desk as patiently as I could while the clock ticked slowly. I could barely manage to work at all. When she finally arrived, I asked her to come into my office and close the door behind her. I burst into tears and immediately told her that my birth family had found me the day before. I spent the rest of the day telling my co-workers about the event, recounting word-for-word my conversations with Elaine and Liz. They were all excited for me and eager to meet my birth mother. I knew how they felt because they were almost as excited as I was. I hadn't even spoken to her yet, and I could only imagine the moment when I'd finally get to meet her, when I'd get to see her face-to-face for the very first time.

The whole time I waited for Vanessa's call, I couldn't think straight. Forgetting about my finals, I worried that she might never call me, since she didn't want to find me in the first place. Time seemed to pass with eternal slowness, and I felt like I lived in a vacuum. The pressure in my head nearly made me explode in frustration. At school, I would tell classmates what had happened, and then burst into tears. I continued to work but could barely maintain my duties with my head in the clouds as I thought about my birth mother. Part of me resented her for not calling sooner. I could only think about how I would feel if I'd found her like I planned—a little strep throat would hardly keep me away, let alone stop me from making a phone call just to hear her voice. I felt lonely during those days of waiting, like she'd rejected me again before I had a chance to even talk to her. I don't think any other days before or since lasted so long. I finally convinced myself that since a lifetime had already passed, a few more days could hardly make a difference. She was ill and I was impatient.

After four days, when I finally heard her voice on the other end of the line, asking, "Is Kasey there?" I felt a peace come over me. Her voice sounded sweet and soft. It tickled my ear, the sound of my birth mother. For a moment, I felt like the infant who longed to hear the beating of her heart against my ear. She sounded nervous. Could she possibly feel as nervous as I felt? She said, "Hi," with a long pause before and after. My immediate impulse was to fill up the pause with my own babble, but I contained myself. I savored even the silence of her presence. We had the conversation I'd wanted to have forever, the one where we told each other how we'd thought about each other all this time.

I told her how I never enjoyed my birthdays and she said she felt the same way. I'd never thought that day would upset her too. But of course it did. That date was also a day of mourning for her, a reminder of the day we'd been separated. The same day I'd spent missing her, she'd also spent missing me. I was secretly happy to learn that I wasn't alone. We talked about my life and my acting career, and it turned out that my feature film was also one of her favorite movies as well. She couldn't believe that every time she had watched that movie, she'd been watching her own daughter and hadn't even known it.

She suggested we meet the following afternoon, a Saturday. I thought waiting a whole day seemed an awfully long time. I wanted to see her that night, that moment! But I acquiesced. I didn't want to unintentionally scare her away. We settled on a quaint little park in the Valley and described ourselves to each other so we could recognize one another. It seemed a little strange that mother and daughter had to say what they looked like so they could find each other in a crowd. Somehow I knew I would easily identify her, regardless. When she described herself, I could hear the resemblances—the long brown hair, the medium frame like mine, one that would never hold the nineteen-inch waist that my adoptive mother had tried so hard to achieve in me.

After she hung up, I tried in vain to go to sleep. Instead I called everyone in my phone book to share the good news, and ended up with strep throat myself. Later Vanessa told me what she had done after that call, how she had gone to four different video stores to find a copy of my movie because each store was out of it. When she finally found a copy, she called Liz and they stayed up till one in the morning watching their favorite movie with new enthusiasm.

A miracle had occurred! There was a God. How could I doubt it?

Chapter 5

Honeymoon

When Saturday dawned, despite the fact that I had woken up sick, I was about to burst from anticipation. The weather had turned cool, and the sky was clear blue without a cloud in sight. The sun shone just warm enough that I needed only a light jacket as I walked through the park. I'd visited this particular park before, and always enjoyed the beauty of the surroundings. The bright, contrasting colors of the flowers and the quiet, peaceful atmosphere soothed the romantic in me. Besides the numerous flowers of every color imaginable, tiny rivers and waterfalls sprinkled the grounds, accentuating the beauty. With the warm climate of Los Angeles, there were always flowers in bloom, a constant rainbow of fresh living color.

Vanessa and I were to meet at three p.m. at the entrance to the park. I arrived early and waited for what seemed an eternity for a five-foot-four, medium-built woman with brown hair to walk up to me. I waited as patiently as I could to finally look into the

face of another and see my own eyes staring back. I
could only imagine what it might feel like. My mind
raced as all those old fantasies and dreams of a scared
five-year-old girl came flooding back. How could
anyone live up to the expectations I'd harbored for
years? I could only hope and pray she'd be as excited to
meet me as I was to meet her.

I thought I spotted her as she drove into the parking
lot. In that perfect moment, her beauty moved me. I
watched her from afar for a time before I got up to walk
toward her. I didn't want to disturb such a beautiful
vision. I took a mental picture and locked it away
forever, something that could be mine and mine alone.
I knew that as long as I lived, I would never forget how
she looked that day at that exact moment. She walked
up slowly, like a scared animal unsure of what to do
around a strange person. She hesitated only a second
before she asked gingerly, "Kasey?"

"Yes," I said. It came out as an exhale that had been
held in a moment too long. I was proud of myself for
not bursting immediately into tears. Then I hugged her,
and nothing ever felt so exquisite. I don't think I could
possibly explain what it felt like to hold against me
the mother I had dreamt about so often, indeed had
fantasized about to the point of obsession. I knew for
the first time in my life the experience of flesh against
my own that shared a common blood. Finally, I felt the
heartbeat from so long ago. It took my breath away, and
I will never forget it. I didn't want to let go, but I was
afraid I might scare her off. That same fear always

prevented me from showing too much emotion around men lest they walk away forever. I was ecstatic to be with Vanessa at last, but in the back of my mind I was consciously taking note of everything I said, every move I made, as I feared I might inadvertently do something wrong that would make her turn and walk away again, this time into oblivion.

We walked to a quiet area of the park and sat down on a bench under some trees. So far, everything had been small talk. We discussed medical issues and discovered that we share many physical ailments, including migraine headaches, TMJ, and vertigo. She told me there was diabetes and breast cancer in my family, diseases I should have known about long ago, especially the diabetes.

After talking about life in general, we showed each other pictures to help catch up on each other's lives. I showed her pictures of me from childhood and adulthood, and she showed me pictures of herself and my birth father, Jeffrey. She assured me that when I was born, she loved Jeffrey very much. Finally, I heard the words that I longed to hear my entire life, that my parents loved each other. She proceeded to tell me all the places they used to go when they were dating, their favorite romantic spot being this very park. It was very comforting to hear that I had walked in the same place as my parents, even though it was a different time. I picked up the picture of her and my father and took a closer look at the people who had brought me into the world. So much time had passed, so many things had transpired. The two in the picture had lived in a completely different time and place. When all the pictures had been brought out and all the small talk was done, we moved on to the deeper part of the conversation: the story of how I was created.

I guess I'll start at the beginning," Vanessa said. "Your father, Jeffrey, was twenty-one and a full-time student. He attended college in the San Fernando Valley. I was a student too, and we worked together at a local bookstore. I was nineteen at the time. We were very much in love and had plans to get married, though we didn't quite know when.

"I became pregnant with you in January of 1967, and our wedding plans became a speedy reality. When I realized I'd become pregnant, I shared the news with Jeffrey. I became scared at the thought of the unknown changes that awaited my body. Jeffrey had suggested adoption as a possible option for us. He said he would do whatever I wanted, that I had to make the ultimate decision. I felt lost, unsure of what to do, and it didn't help that Jeffrey never voiced any concern or genuine opinion of desire either way. To me, he seemed very indifferent, as if our decision to keep you or give you away had the same significance as choosing between a burger from McDonald's or Carl's Jr. Five words summed up the extent of his support: 'Hey, it's up to you.'

"Even in the late 1960s during the heyday of the sexual revolution and free love, a single pregnant girl was considered 'in trouble.' Jeffrey and I, both Episcopalians, were raised in a church with very stringent beliefs against pre-marital sex and divorce. Your father had already been married, had a daughter, and gone through a divorce. Because of his divorce, our request to marry in the Episcopalian church was refused, so we were married by a non-denominational minister on March 19, 1967, in your grandmother's home."

So I was at my parents' wedding. I was hiding in her womb, an invisible witness to the vows of eternity they made to each other, a secret gift of love that only they knew about.

"It wasn't until after the wedding, after the honeymoon had come and gone, that we decided to announce the pregnancy. But we told everyone that I was newly pregnant, rather than let them know about the careless mistake I had made and that we had married so quickly because of you. Everyone thought we were a young couple about to build a family. No one knew the plans we had made."

I wanted to ask her how she got away with telling everybody that she had only just gotten pregnant. Didn't people figure out that she was farther along in her pregnancy because of the size of her stomach?

She continued, "Jeffrey and I began relinquishment proceedings with the adoption agency on August 14, 1967, two months before you were born. I was sure that my parents would never accept the idea that I became pregnant before marrying your father. In fact, I desperately feared that the family would disown me if they found out. I also knew that we hadn't yet reached the proper time in our lives to have children. We were still too young. We simply decided we weren't prepared to deal with the responsibilities of raising a child so early in our marriage."

I wanted to tell her that I disagreed with her reasoning. After all, didn't she get married in order to avoid being labeled "a single girl in trouble"? I chose to hear her out.

"I went into labor at five a.m. on October 12, 1967. We went to the hospital alone; in fact, Jeffrey just dropped me off at the front door. Since we planned to give you up, we purposely didn't notify any family members that I had gone into labor. We didn't want anyone around who would then learn the truth."

I couldn't believe it. For my birth, no one attended. It was literally empty in the waiting room. No anxious relatives showed up to wait and hope for a healthy and happy baby. My father didn't pace back and forth outside the birthing room, eagerly awaiting my arrival. What kind of man would simply drop off his pregnant wife at the hospital door when she was about to give birth to his child?

But there was more. She continued, "I stayed awake

during most of the labor, though I was administered drugs for the pain. I had actually fallen asleep after I delivered you into the world. I gave birth to you at 3:07 p.m. You weighed in at six pounds, fifteen ounces, and measured twenty inches long. But before I could see you or hold you, the nurse, who knew I was going to give you up for adoption, removed you from the birthing room before I woke up.

"The next day, I pleaded with the nurses to bring you to me so I could hold you in my arms. But the hospital had a policy that if I was giving you up for adoption, they wouldn't allow me to hold you in order to prevent us from bonding. I can vividly recall myself standing on the other side of the nursery room window, with my fingers spread against the glass, in an effort to get just a millimeter nearer to you."

So that day, I didn't know the feeling of being held against her chest where I could feel her heartbeat and know we were separate and yet one. I knew now that I was not held by my birth mother. Perhaps that would explain my longing for her; I never had a chance to bond with her!

As Vanessa continued the story of my birth, she lowered her voice to a whisper. She seemed awash with a sense of shame as the words came forth describing how she saw me in the hospital, but wasn't allowed to hold me. I thought of the cross she'd had to bear over the years, and the one I had carried myself, as a result of a single moment twenty-seven years before when she and I had been separated.

My birth mother continued, "When I left the hospital two days later, I went to my mother's home to recuperate from what my family thought was a stillborn delivery. I was devastated. Words cannot describe how I yearned for you. I used to wake up in a cold sweat and cry out for you. I didn't get the opportunity to hold you until the following week when Jeffrey and I went to the adoption agency. I felt so alive the moment a woman came into the room carrying you in her arms.

"When I did finally hold you, I had an incredible spiritual experience. It may sound silly to you, but it was the sort of feeling one encounters upon first discovering that there just might be a God, a hope for mankind in a crazy universe. I looked into your eyes in awe, touched your soft face with my hands, and wondered in amazement that my little nineteen-year-old body had produced such a miracle in you. I felt the softness of your skin against my fingertips and listened to the gurgling sounds you made but knew I had to let you go, to forget about you so I wouldn't go crazy with regret. Any emotional attachment would have only made it harder, I knew. But I was your mother and I couldn't help it. It only took a split second for me to fall in love with you beyond description."

What could I say? How could I respond to this story of how she loved me so much and ached for me, yet still felt she couldn't keep me? I thought about how different things are for my generation in the 1990s, and I wanted to say, "Well, you could've changed your mind and said to hell with societal taboos!"

As I thought these thoughts, she explained. "When I held you at the agency that day, I almost changed my mind. In you, I saw a piece of myself and knew that if I gave you up, all that would also disappear. The social worker noticed my ambivalence and asked me if I was sure about my decision, and told me it wasn't too late to change my mind. In that split second I had a moment of hope. I knew that if Jeffrey would give me just one look, no matter how brief, or one touch, or a simple reassuring word, I would feel confident enough to change my mind. But my hope quickly faded when I turned to him, wishing he might have the same look of joy upon his own face, and found instead a look of stoic indifference.

"Even so, I didn't want to give you back to the social worker. I wanted to keep you and take you home, to forget about the whole charade and make of our lives what we could. But now, I felt as if I didn't have a choice, that the decision had finally carved itself in stone unchangeably. I thought about what my family would say. I was sure they would disown me if they knew I'd gotten pregnant two months earlier than they thought. I told myself that I couldn't suddenly appear with a baby girl in my arms, after telling them you were stillborn. I knew I had to make a decision. A thousand thoughts ran through my head—family, Jeffrey, my future, you—and in the end, of course, I felt I had no choice but to go through with it.

"Later, I asked for a picture of you and a letter

describing your adoptive family. They sent me this picture. I received it just before I signed the final relinquishment papers." She handed me the picture. I was being held by a nameless, faceless social worker, and I looked so scared! "I need to tell you that not a day went by when I didn't think about you and look at this picture. You may keep it if you'd like."

I was amazed at how an innocent picture of me taken twenty-seven years earlier would bring up such sadness. The feelings were profound. I obviously had no recollection of the picture being taken, but when I saw it while sitting next to my birth mother it sent chills down my spine. As I look back to that day, remembering what all those books I had read talked about, it all makes perfect sense that the bonding between mother and child, even before birth, is a powerful, soulful connection. And if babies can recognize their mother's face and even seek out their mother, then of course I must have been sad and scared that she was suddenly missing.

Vanessa continued her story in clinical detail. She told me dates and times and offices that she and Jeffrey had visited to complete the relinquishment transaction. She detached herself a bit as she related how she signed "under care" papers, which placed me in the foster care system. On November 15, 1967, they signed the final papers that released me for adoption.

"I want to explain to you why I never searched for you myself," she continued. "I felt I'd given up all rights to you when I signed the relinquishment papers back in 1967. I wanted to make it your decision to find me if that's what you wanted." Though I didn't necessarily understand her reasoning, I tried to accept it. Thank God that Elaine and Liz had persisted, I thought to myself. Thank God they had found me and given me the moment Vanessa and I had together that day.

As I sat there and listened to Vanessa relive the days that surrounded my birth, I couldn't help but wonder if she had ever imagined that she would someday sit with her adult daughter, the one she gave away, and have to explain what had gone on in her head when she had made that decision. Had she hoped she would never have to tell me her family thought I was dead? Would she have done anything different? Or had she known all along that this day would come? I wondered if it helped her or hurt her to have to do this now, when it was her mother and sister, Elaine and Liz, who were the driving force behind the search for me.

I had a hard time understanding some of the things Vanessa told me, though I tried my best to remain nonjudgmental and unbiased. I could hardly relate to a young girl in the 1960s who gave up her child for adoption because she worried about what her parents would think. Compared to the generation I grew up in, becoming pregnant two months before marriage seemed almost a positive. Nevertheless, that was the story she told me, and I made every attempt to comprehend the things I now knew.

It shocked me to hear how they had informed both

families that she had lost the baby. It stunned me that throughout my entire life, most of my birth family hadn't even known I'd existed, even to this day. It seemed so much more the miracle that Elaine and Liz had eventually found me, than the fact that I was sitting in the park that day on a wooden bench under a sparse green tree meeting with the same mother who had allowed everyone to think I was dead.

When Vanessa finished her story, she asked me if I was angry with her. I told her no, though I later realized that I really had been. I wanted to tell her then about all my fantasies and nightmares regarding why I was given up. I wanted to tell her that I was convinced my birth parents could not have been married, because married couples don't give up their children. I had so many reasons to explode, to tell her everything I felt I'd suffered since the day she let me go. On the other hand, I knew the value of forgiveness. Mostly, it saddened me to think I had spent my life without her, especially when I considered how unhappy I'd been in my adoptive home.

She apologized for whatever pain her decision had caused me, and I believed that she was sorry. Though I had trouble forgiving her, for the moment I decided not to yell at her for letting Jeffrey bamboozle her into giving me up. I held back my desire to tell her that she had the choice, societal pressures or not, that she was the one who made the final decision. I bit my tongue when I learned that most of my family didn't even know I existed.

She also didn't yet need to know exactly how much pain I had endured in the years of our separation. How would she have reacted in that moment if she knew Todd had molested me and attempted to drown me? Or if she knew how unloved I felt by my adoptive mother? Would she accept me if she knew how I had drowned myself in excess food, alcohol, and marijuana? Worst of all, how much would she blame herself if she knew how much hatred and loathing I had always experienced, not directed at her but at myself?

As I squelched my sadness at learning the bitter truth of the circumstances of my relinquishment, I tried to focus on the positive. Vanessa showed me more pictures of Jeffrey, and again I saw my own facial features captured in the emulsion of photograph after photograph. The resemblance stunned me. The similarities struck me harder than they had even in the first moment I had glimpsed Vanessa as she arrived at the park earlier that day. I had her body, but I had his face. Vanessa looked closely at one of the pictures of Jeffrey. "You have his eyes," she said softly, "his beautiful green eyes."

As we sat in the park that day, the afternoon becoming more and more cool with the passing hours, we tried to catch up with one another. It was impossible to do. Too many years had passed. I wanted her to know everything about me and didn't know where to start. I wanted her to know each detail, from what it had felt like the first time a bee had stung me to the horrors I'd endured in the years of Todd's abuse. I steered away from the bad parts, in truth, because I didn't know how she would deal with me. And I think the little girl in me was scared to death that she would think there was something wrong with me and would go away, never to return.

She had a right to know about all that had happened and all I had experienced, and I wanted her to know. But for the moment, I would have to wait. I told myself I would share everything with her eventually. Someday, when I mustered enough courage. But for now, it pleased me just to know her, to love her, and to look at her beautiful smile I had inherited. I reveled in the appreciation I had for the similar shape of our bodies, something I'd always longed to see as a child. An understanding slowly settled in on me that other people in the world also had hips and meat on their bones. Despite the constant criticism I felt I'd received from my adoptive mother, I wasn't a freak of nature. I was born from love, and now I knew that Vanessa and Jeffrey had released me because of fear, not because they didn't love me.

As we made our way to the parking lot, I asked a man walking by to take a picture of Vanessa and me. Little did he know that he was the first person ever to take a picture of mother and daughter together. We made plans to meet the rest of the Geiger clan the next day at Elaine's house in Chatsworth, the house where my parents had married. Vanessa told me she didn't know Jeffrey's whereabouts anymore, and at this point

I really didn't care. I only wanted my mother, and finally, I had her.

The next day, I pulled up in front of a moderate-sized blue house in Chatsworth. I smiled as I remembered that my apartment was only down the street while I attended CSUN in my early twenties. I sat in the car for a moment before I went in and tried to prepare myself for the experience I never imagined would happen. In moments, I would meet three extended-family members for the first time. I would see my mother again, the one I had so quickly come to love only the day before, and I couldn't wait to experience her side of the family.

Vanessa greeted me at the door. I felt nervous to say the least. Meeting her had been one thing, but being thrown into a completely new family was something else entirely. All my emotions began to creep up, the ones that told me to worry about what they would think, how they saw me, and if I was doing everything right. As it turned out, I needn't have worried.

My aunt Liz, grandmother Elaine, and uncle Mark were behind her at the door. It seemed like a scene from a movie as they stood there and stared back at me through the doorway, smiles across all of their faces. We said our obligatory hellos and I hugged each of them nervously as they ushered me into the living room. As I settled into Elaine's home, I felt as if I had stepped into yet another new chapter of my life.

We moved into the kitchen and went into another round of questions and answers. We looked at childhood pictures of me that I had brought, and we looked through all of their family photo albums. In picture after picture, I saw parts of me like I had never seen them before. In one I saw my funny-shaped knees, in another my thick brown hair. In one grinning face after another I recognized my own smile, and the green eyes and thick eyebrows that had benefited me as a child actress. As I saw those pictures, I understood for the first time why my adoptive mother could never succeed in dieting me down to a nineteen-inch waist—it would have been against the laws of nature, against the alphanumeric code of my genetics. Because before me I saw aunts, cousins, and other female relatives of average weight who had average-sized waistlines. What a gift it was for me to see myself among them, and to accept the fact that if they looked perfectly normal, then so did I. They commented on my similar gestures and mannerisms. I even walked like Vanessa. I never knew I did anything like anyone. Finally, I found my link to the world.

Six hours later we decided to go out for dinner and opted for Chinese. During the dinner my birth family gave me a beautiful velvet box to help commemorate our first meeting. Inside it sat a crystal, a symbol of the spiritual bonding that occurred from the gathering that night. Later, I put in my own memento, a pendant inscribed with a single date, 1994, because I never wanted to forget that year, the year I became born again into my birth family.

When we returned to the house, we viewed an old tape of Jeffrey and Vanessa's wedding, and I watched in wonder at the scene where I had been while still in the womb of my mother. I'd hid inside her while no one else knew. If only I'd known then how my existence would remain a secret to many for nearly thirty years.

I felt comfortable with my new relatives, and glad that I did. I thought it would have felt horrible had I gone to meet them only to find we had nothing in common and didn't like each other. We laughed together a lot and Liz brought out her camcorder to videotape us as we played charades. It was something corny I would have done with my own friends and it made me ecstatic to see they enjoyed the same sort of things I did.

I left at eleven p.m., exhausted from the weekend of discovery I had experienced. I took my final exams the following week and passed with flying colors.

I returned again on Christmas day, when everyone gathered together at Elaine's house. This time we were joined by my younger brother, Adam. Though I had grown up with two adoptive brothers and thought I knew what brothers were all about, it still excited me to meet Adam and find out what my birth brother was like.

Liz was not there because she needed to get back to

Monterey to be with her husband, James, and their ailing dog, Stu. Mark, Elaine, Vanessa, Adam, and I sat around exchanging gifts and talked about what a miracle it was for me to be spending Christmas day with them. They all showered me with gifts, and I gave Vanessa a framed picture of us from the day we met, two weeks before.

My twenty-year-old brother, Adam, touched me deeply when he gave me a homemade photo album of him growing up so I could see what I had missed. He told me repeatedly that he was so excited to know he had a sister. It was fascinating to discover that in addition to the physical characteristics Adam and I shared, we had many other things in common. We both worked at a retirement home for years, and unfortunately, we both had the predisposition to use substances to excess. He was very much into partying and found every opportunity to recount play-by-play what happened when he got drunk, which was often. And while I saw myself in his stories, it was difficult for me to hear them. Still, we shared a bond of being born of the same woman, and I am his only sister, his only sibling. This I will always treasure.

That year, I spent New Year's Eve with Vanessa. I went to her home in Woodland Hills for the first time. We went out to dinner and continued our journey to get to know each other better. It pleased me to find she didn't like wild parties or late nights. Since I quit drinking, I felt the same way and preferred a quiet evening at home to one out on the town. We relaxed at her house and I left at ten-thirty, an hour and a half before the new year rang in.

She walked me to my car and we hugged again. People do this all the time, but it felt marvelously exquisite to me. I knew in that instant how much I loved her, in spite of all that had happened. I wanted to tell her, but was afraid to do so at the same time. A part of me said, "I don't know her well enough yet," while the other part of me said, "It doesn't matter—she's your mother." I knew she loved me by the way she looked at me, watched me, and followed my car with her eyes as I drove off. I wondered if, like me, she feared her own emotions, the way she felt so deeply for another being.

On February 12, 1995, my adoptive father and Kimberly threw me a "meet the birth family" party. I never thought I would see the day when members of my adoptive family and birth family would be sitting in the same room. I will never forget the moment when I introduced my adoptive father to my birth mother Vanessa, my birth grandmother Elaine, and my birth uncle Mark. It was as if we were old friends. We laughed, played games, and talked about what a miracle it was that we were all together.

The next time I saw my birth family was one month later when Elaine moved to Monterey to live closer to Liz and James. It was when Elaine was preparing for the move that I received a precious gift, a dresser that

Vanessa had as a child. Elaine wanted me to have it, a sort of memento, a part of Vanessa's history. Needless to say, I treasured my new dresser.

I found it sadly ironic that after Elaine planned for years to find me, by the time she did, she had already made plans to move up north. But before she moved, she wanted me to learn the story of how she discovered I was alive and how she found me almost three decades later.

"Two days after you were born, I got a horrifying call from Jeffrey telling me that Vanessa had 'lost the baby.' I couldn't figure out why he hadn't told anyone that Vanessa had even gone into labor, and especially why he would wait two full days before letting anyone know what had happened. I thought such a tragic event would at least warrant an immediate phone call. It seemed extremely unusual that Jeffrey would casually make the phone call forty-eight hours later. I asked Jeffrey if he had made the funeral arrangements. Jeffrey's reply was that the hospital would take care of the arrangements. Since I was a nurse, I knew that all deaths were given the same treatment and respect. I knew from experience that hospitals never take care of funeral or burial arrangements. It was always the family's responsibility. I felt certain that you were alive somewhere and that they'd given you up for adoption. I felt angry, sad, and betrayed. I asked myself how my daughter could do such a thing and lie to the family, saying you had died. Most of all, I couldn't understand why Vanessa hadn't come to me first to tell me about the pregnancy. I desperately wanted to come right out and say it, to look my daughter in the eye and ask, 'Did you give the baby up?' But I was afraid. I suppose I really didn't want to know the answer.

"In October of 1968, I decided to change hospitals and was pleased to learn that there was a job opening in the maternity ward of the hospital where Vanessa gave birth to you. I applied for the position and was hired on the spot. Ironically, my first day on the job was October 12, 1968—your first birthday! I had made up my mind before I even arrived that I would locate Vanessa's file and find out what had really happened to you. I decided I had to know, no matter what the consequences.

"It didn't take long for me to find my way around the hospital and familiarize myself with places like the records room. I quickly retrieved Vanessa's chart, opened it, and found Vanessa's signature giving the hospital permission to relinquish you to the adoption agency. I was shocked. I'd had suspicions all along, since the very day I had received that phone call from your father. But to see the truth there in the file, written down in black and white, made it all a painful reality.

"I went home and immediately told my husband, Nathaniel, what I had discovered. I begged him to go with me to confront Vanessa and together we went directly to Vanessa and Jeffrey's apartment. It took all I had to restrain myself. We all sat down and I looked Vanessa in the eye and told her I knew exactly what had happened. I said to her, 'You went into that hospital, you had that baby, and you gave her up for adoption, didn't you!' Vanessa told me how it had terrified her to think that I would disown her if I found out she'd become pregnant before she and Jeffrey had married. She said she thought the family would ostracize her. I couldn't understand my daughter's fears. After all, we had known about the pregnancy anyway, regardless of when the actual conception had occurred. It all seemed unconscionable to me, the way Vanessa could give you away and then tell the family she'd lost you.

"Mark was still in Vietnam when he got the news that you were given away, but no one told Liz that you were alive until some years later. Liz had been excited at the prospect of a brand-new niece or nephew, and when we told her you had died, it saddened her horribly. She knew something was wrong when she noticed how cold I had become toward Vanessa. My behavior puzzled her because we had supposedly lost a family member, and yet instead of grieving, I had become enraged. Through those first years, she would periodically ask what the problem was between Vanessa and myself, but because we felt she was too young to understand, she never got a straight answer. We finally decided to tell her when she turned seventeen. Now she finally understood my anger at Vanessa.

"Like me, Liz had problems understanding why Vanessa had given you away. After all, she and Jeffrey were married. But unlike me, Liz felt more curious about what Vanessa had done rather than being mad at her. Since she didn't seem to understand the complexity of what had transpired, she just assumed Vanessa must have had a good reason for doing what she did.

"Five years later, Liz began to ask Vanessa if she ever thought about you. By this time, Liz had built up quite a little fantasy about you in her own mind. She wondered for hours about what kind of person you were becoming, and wished that none of this had ever happened so she wouldn't have to wonder at all. She used to come to me with ideas of finding out where you went to school so she could park outside the playground and watch you with the other children, as you skipped rope or chanted out some schoolgirl rhyme. Liz and I thought of what you looked like and how you must resemble Vanessa, and perhaps even ourselves. Or would you look more like Jeffrey with his brown hair and striking green eyes? Since the moment we told Liz of your fate, she wanted to find you. She dreamed of the day she could look her niece in the eye and say, 'I have thought about you always.'

"When you were seven, the birth of your half brother, Adam, proved to be a welcome distraction for us from thoughts of missing you. Since neither Liz nor Mark ever had any children of their own, there was finally a grandchild in the house. For all intents and purposes, we had to consider you permanently out of the picture, so Adam became the only grandchild. We focused on him. We adored him and loved him the way one should love a baby. He smiled in Vanessa's arms as we took photographs; he ripped bright shiny paper from his first Christmas presents as ecstatic eyes looked on in wonderment. In short, the world that became his is the one you missed out on, that I suppose you will never have the opportunity to experience or relive.

"Eventually, your existence haunted Liz and me again. After all, we could hardly deny or forget that another grandchild existed somewhere, a sister for Adam whose rightful place was smiling next to the beautiful baby boy in all those pictures that we took. Throughout the family, an underlying feeling of apprehension tainted any good fortune that we encountered, because no matter how well things might go, or how perfect they might seem, we knew the truth —that one of us, our own flesh and blood, remained missing.

"I especially thought of you on your birthday and hoped you were having a wonderful celebration of your entrance into this life. At one point, I made a decision to find you before I died. I thought of searching for you when you were in elementary school, then again when you were in high school. But when the idea of a search tempted me, I backed off. I didn't want to cause upset to your adoptive family. I ultimately decided to wait until enough years had passed that you would have left home. That way, I wouldn't need to worry about your adoptive parents. I was concerned about what they might think or do, especially if they had never told you that you were adopted.

"By the time you became old enough, we had to consider Adam, who did not know that you existed. Liz and I decided we would begin to look for you once Adam became an adult. Our search would begin with or without Vanessa's consent. So when Adam finally turned eighteen, Liz urged Vanessa to tell him he had a sister. She didn't.

"The next year, Liz took the now nineteen-year-old Adam aside. She wanted desperately to tell him everything she knew about you, sure he would share in the elation that she herself had experienced upon discovering your existence. She told Adam there were things about his family that he should know and had a right to know, in effect planting a seed of curiosity in his mind. But she didn't launch into a full-scale exposition about you. Instead, she pushed Adam toward his mother and forced Vanessa to tell him the truth. Once Adam knew, nothing could hold back Liz and myself from beginning our search for you. After twenty-six years of thinking about you and wanting to find you, it seemed like a new part of life had opened up for both of us, especially myself. Now, finally, we had crossed the last hurdle. Nothing could stop us. Liz and I decided to begin our search immediately.

"In July of 1994, when I was seventy-nine, Liz and I decided to register with ALMA in hopes that you had registered as well."

How amazing, that they started their search only three months before I began gathering search resources. In fact, I had the same literature from ALMA—the Adoptee's Liberty Movement Association—sitting on my desk at home, but I had never bothered to register with them. After all, I wasn't going to officially start my search until June of 1997. Had I taken the time to fill out the simple paperwork, I would have been reunited with my birth family months earlier.

Elaine continued, "I contacted a doctor I knew and asked him for advice on how to locate my long-lost granddaughter. He referred me to four different search specialists. I felt confident that a specialist would find you, and I didn't care how much money it would cost. I'd seen all those television shows about detectives where there was a down payment, a retainer, expenses, etc. I thought it would probably cost a small fortune, but that didn't daunt me. I plowed on, determined to find you. I called each of the names and after hiring a specialist, it surprised me to learn that the search would take about two months.

"On the morning of December 5, 1994, after many barriers in the search, my specialist called and suggested that I contact Dr. Belman, an obstetrician and former colleague of mine. He practiced in the same hospital you were born in. I was instructed to ask if he could possibly obtain your chart from the records room, the same chart that I had located back in 1968. I was excited at the possibility and I called him right away. Though Dr. Belman wanted to help, he was unable to locate the file because at the time, the hospital destroyed all charts after eighteen years. I was crushed. It seemed every avenue had quickly become a dead end until Dr. Belman called again later that same day.

"My breath caught in my throat when I heard him say he'd found out the names of the people who had adopted you, and that they had named you Kasey. At that point, I didn't care how he found out or what laws he had to break. In fact, I didn't even ask. I was simply thrilled to know that a Mr. and Mrs. Pat Hamner raised my beloved granddaughter.

"Finally, after all these years, after all the thoughts and dreams I had about you and where you lived, I knew your name. Though you had already reached adulthood when I heard your name for the very first time, for me it was as if you had just been born.

"Not only did Dr. Belman know your name, he'd discovered from old adoption records the address and phone number of your adoptive parents in Beverly Hills."

Amazingly, the address and phone number were still accurate, as twenty-seven years later my adoptive mother still lived in the same house.

She continued, "Though I was happy to receive the information, I suddenly felt at a loss to take action. I called Dr. Belman and asked him what I should do. He suggested I call your adoptive parents directly, but I didn't want to upset them. I decided that since you were now twenty-seven, and most likely lived on your own, it would be best to call you directly. I tried to look up your name in the telephone book. It amazed me that all these years, your number could have been listed there, sitting in this huge book on my kitchen counter.

I just never knew which name to look under. But now I knew. I turned to the page for Hamner, but out of a handful of Hamners listed, I couldn't find a listing for Kasey or K. I did find a disconnected number for a P. Hamner."

I thought to myself that perhaps she called the number for my brother Peter, who had recently moved to South Carolina.

"But I called directory assistance and got another area listing for the last name Hamner. I called and got a kooky man on the phone who claimed not to know you but asked if the call was in regards to an acting job.

"After this second dead end, I called directory assistance again and explained to the operator that I needed to locate K. Hamner in Los Angeles. Thankfully, the operator helped immensely. She searched the entire greater Los Angeles area and finally turned up a phone number in Glendale."

The rest is history.

Now Elaine was moving away, and I knew I would miss her immensely. I could always drive six hours to see her, but part of me wished she would stay right here in Chatsworth. With disappointment in my heart, I rode up to Monterey with Vanessa and Mark to assist Elaine with the move.

I stayed with Liz and James in their beautiful house where I felt immediately comfortable. I'd grown up in and around Los Angeles, and it was a completely different environment that I found myself in, in northern California, in the middle of nowhere, in this big house next to a huge plot of land with its own pond. At night, the frogs serenaded us. From outside, they sounded deafening, especially to a big-city girl like me. I wished I could have stayed longer. I only had time to get Elaine moved and settled into her new condo, but I knew that I would come back many times in the near future. I was pleased to be of service to the woman who had so diligently searched for me until she found me. I made plans to return soon and stay longer.

The next month, I invited Vanessa to come to the retirement home where I worked so she could see what I did with my life and meet my co-workers. They were eager to meet her and I wanted to show off my beautiful mother to everyone I knew. They all enjoyed meeting her and she even accompanied me on our annual company cruise to Catalina Island the following June. It must have been an extraordinary sight witnessing both of us up on the deck of the ferry, faces turned defiantly into the wind as we tried not to throw up. "Like mother, like daughter," I thought, and the words sounded strange and new to my mind.

My adoptive mother said it pleased her that I had reunited with my birth family. I wonder, though, if her comment was based merely on the fear that I would finally desert her for my birth mother, as I had threatened to do so many times as an angry young girl. I wondered if she was really mad at me for even being involved with my birth family, secretly hoping that the reunion never occurred. She asked if she could meet Vanessa and I was surprised, to say the least. I assumed it would be too hard for my adoptive mother to see the biological relationship and all the similarities between us. Nevertheless, the two of us showed up at her home, the home I grew up in, one afternoon in late March of 1995.

When my adoptive mother opened the door to greet us, the first thing she said was, "Well Kasey, I certainly don't like your hair today!" I attempted to smile through my embarrassment. I had to remind myself that we were there because I wanted nothing more than for Vanessa to see where I had grown up. I wanted Vanessa to see the bedroom where I'd lain in my bed at night as I cried for her, and the backyard where I'd played for hours with the dogs who for a time filled my life with happiness and distracted me from thoughts of her. I showed her the elementary school a mile from the house, but omitted stories of sneaking away to the store where I would steal candy bars to binge on later in secret.

It felt strange to visit that house with her, to show her photo albums of my adoptive family that my adoptive mother had put together in chronological order. It thrilled me to show her all the pictures of me as a child, but they reminded me of all the bad times I had yet to tell her about. Being in that place was like walking through a house of horrors, with a myriad of ghosts that stood up, screeching to be heard as I showed Vanessa the photographs of my youth that she had not been present to see. As I looked at those pictures for the first time in years, I realized that I wasn't as fat as I'd always thought when I was growing up. In those books sat the truth, the proof I'd refused to allow myself to see; instead I had believed my adoptive mother and put myself down time and time again.

The three of us gathered in the living room on the couch that was only to be sat on during special occasions. My adoptive mother expressed to Vanessa what a joy I was to raise and I felt torn by conflicting realities. Old feelings arose again, reminding me of my childhood when my adoptive mother would sing my praises in front of company, only to alienate me later at home when she would treat me like the maid. Resentment began to rear its head again as it had when all the other children played outside while I stayed locked away inside doing the laundry and other chores. Years later, I would feel the same way when I lived there as a college student and had to ask her permission to use the washer and dryer and she would get upset at me for doing more than one load a week.

I had never felt comfortable in that home. I'd always felt like an outsider, the maid, and that day was no exception. I felt guilty because I wanted to show Vanessa the pictures and leave before I would have to experience what I felt was false sincerity from my adoptive mother. I held my tongue and remained calm because Vanessa didn't know the history between my adoptive mother and me, and I wasn't ready to tell her.

Vanessa seemed to enjoy my adoptive mother's stories about how cute I'd looked on television and how well I'd performed in school. I kept saying to myself, "Why didn't she ever tell me that?" All the time I'd grown up there, I felt plagued by feelings of inadequacy, that I was never good enough or smart enough, and certainly never beautiful or cute enough. And here was my adoptive mother, singing songs of praise as if she had always thought I exemplified perfection. Part of me felt grateful that she painted such a flattering portrait of me, but another part wanted to scream and yell at her and ask why she'd never been able to tell me those things when I was scared and uncertain and needed the compliments so much more. When Vanessa and I were alone, the truth would eventually come out. But now was not the time.

Finally, the uncomfortable reunion of mothers and daughter concluded. It couldn't have ended too soon. My adoptive mother smiled, overly nice to both of us, and told Vanessa how much she enjoyed meeting her. She invited us to come back anytime. As we left the house, Vanessa thanked my adoptive mother for doing such a good job of raising me. As my adoptive mother graciously replied, "You're so welcome," I wanted to

scream from the top of my lungs and tell Vanessa that
my success had more to do with my genetic package
and self-determination. Despite my adoptive mother's
wishes, we would never return to that house in Beverly
Hills.

I spent most of the summer of 1995 enjoying the
presence of this new family in my life. On the Fourth
of July, I drove alone to Monterey to spend quality time
with Liz and Elaine. Liz and I went on hikes and long
walks. We went shopping at the local mall and she
taught me how to canoe in her pond. We stayed up
until all hours of the night while we talked and shared
secrets, just like junior high school girls.

Adam had come down to Monterey from school and
the two of us drove thirty miles to the nearest fireworks
show at a high school. We didn't want to pay the
outrageous fee to get into the stadium, so we sat behind
the stage to watch the fireworks and got to know each
other. As he pulled a can of beer out of his jacket pocket
and lit up a joint, he asked me not to tell our mother
what he was doing and proceeded to tell me about his
latest drinking escapades. I attempted to change the
subject and discuss more thought-provoking topics
such as family and reunion. He wanted no part of that
conversation. He became very evasive with me and I
saw for the first time a great deal of sadness and rage in

him. I realized I was not going to get far in trying to know the "real" Adam, so I let him do the talking.

He asked how long it had been since I had a drink and when I said over five years, he told me that I must lead a boring existence without it. It would have been a waste of time telling him how full my life was. Because in Adam's eyes, not drinking was equated with boredom. If only he could hear the truth about where he was headed if he continued down the road he was on. But I knew that telling him how to live his life was none of my business and would only fall on deaf ears anyway. I told him that if he ever decided that he didn't want to drink or use drugs anymore, I would be there for him. At that point, all I could do was teach by example.

During the presentation, a fire broke out near the backstage of the fireworks display. My intoxicated brother immediately ran over to the fire and grabbed a hose in a clumsy attempt to put it out. He did not come back until a fireman arrived five minutes later. I was frightened that he would hurt himself, but all I could do was pray, stay put, and wait for him to return. Luckily he was unharmed and we returned to Liz and James's house safely. I did not tell the others what had happened. From that evening on, I began to pray for him, hoping that one day he would come to me for help.

In August, Vanessa went with me to my favorite dance club. I got to introduce her as my mother, and I loved it. Everyone commented on how much we looked alike, and I thought I would never grow tired of hearing that. I found it refreshing, especially since I'd looked nothing like my adoptive mother. Throughout the summer months, Vanessa and I continued to get together. We went to movies and got to know each other, little by little.

My twenty-eighth birthday was my first birthday in this "reunion" phase of my life. I will never forget it. We had a mini family reunion of sorts in Monterey. My adoptive father, my stepmother Kimberly, Vanessa, my uncle Mark, and I drove up from Los Angeles. Elaine now had to drive only two blocks to meet us at Liz and James's house. I never dreamt I would one day celebrate my birthday with my biological and adoptive families at the same time. It felt like such a gift to wander among them and know how much they all loved me. I'd never had a happier birthday. I'd been given the one thing I'd always desperately wanted, the thing I had always wished for as I blew out the candles—my birth mother. Not only did I get that precious gift, but an added surprise of an aunt, two uncles, a half brother, and a grandmother.

The more time I spent with Liz, and the closer we became, the more I had thoughts of moving to Monterey after I finished graduate school. I started to obsess about moving in with my relatives, especially my birth mother, even though she only lived thirty miles from me. I knew it was unrealistic to move in with her, so I fantasized about moving into a guest house that James said he would build for me on their property. I had it all planned out. I'd get a job as a school psychologist at a school district in Monterey and I'd have Sunday dinner every week with my relatives. We'd eat mashed potatoes and steak and I would never worry about how big my waistline was.

In November of 1995, I moved out of my apartment in Glendale, the apartment I'd lived in when I received the call from Elaine. I moved into a disastrous apartment down the street and heard babies crying constantly from the first day I lived there. I'd always valued a quiet place to live, and felt trapped since I couldn't afford to move again so soon. Bernie Fanfield, a platonic dancing buddy of mine, offered me the opportunity to live in his house. He needed some financial assistance to make his mortgage payment and I needed a quiet place to study. It worked out well. He had a beautiful three-bedroom house on top of a hill in Glendale. On a clear day you could see as far as the ocean, thirty miles away. He also had two cats and a dog, an added bonus because in exchange for lower rent, I took care of his animals when he went away on vacation.

I spent that Christmas in Monterey. The family had traditionally gone up there for holidays, and this year, our second Christmas together, I joined them. I really felt like I belonged, like I had found at last the people who would never judge me. Adam, Sarah (a neighbor of Liz and James's), and I went Christmas caroling down the street. We sang off tune, but we didn't care.

Around this time, Liz started to ask me if I wanted to find my birth father, Jeffrey. Each time I gave her an emphatic no. After all, he'd told the family I had died. What would I need him for? She was quiet for a moment, then said one last thing: "If you ever change your mind, I'll help you locate him. If you want to."

In February of 1996, the position of administrator of the retirement home became available. I thought I would be a shoe-in. After all, I'd worked there for four years, had a great reputation with the staff and residents and knew all the ins and outs of the business. I convinced myself that I could handle finishing graduate school and running the retirement home at the same time. The salary increase would come in handy to help me pay my tuition as well. It crushed me when I didn't get the job. They hired somebody else—an outsider who had never worked in a retirement home before. Although I was disappointed, I didn't let that setback destroy me as I once would have. Instead, I left the retirement home and began a counseling internship at a school district that paid five dollars an hour, a huge cut in salary. But I was excited to be working with children and I knew the experience would help me prepare for the field of school psychology.

In June of 1996, I successfully completed two of my three years of graduate school. I was still renting a room from Bernie, was happily taking care of his animals, and found myself heavily immersed in the process of integrating into my new family. I felt I had succeeded rather nicely, except in my relationship with Vanessa. After our initial meeting in December of 1994, then our moviegoing excursions, a visit with my adoptive mother, and a few other social events, our phone calls and get-togethers seemed to diminish with time. I began to realize that Vanessa was never the one to initiate contact or make plans with me. I was always the one to call first. It also struck me that after a year and a half of reunion with her, we were not able to talk about emotional, personal, intimate things. It felt like she was slowly pulling away from me. Our rare conversations centered on impersonal topics like politics and the weather, and whenever the conversation drifted to a sensitive topic that I would have been more than happy to participate in, she would abruptly change the subject. I so wanted a soulful connection with her, but was beginning to see that it was not going to happen.

The longer I knew Vanessa, the more intensely private she became. I also learned, after a year and a half of reunion, that she did not tell any of her friends about me. I hated being kept a secret and asked her why she didn't tell anybody about our reunion. She told me that she was still frightfully ashamed of what she had done and would never tell anybody her horrible secret.

I could not relate to her feelings—I continued to announce my reunion to anybody who would listen. Now it made perfect sense to me why she stopped coming to my parties and get-togethers—she perhaps didn't want to be introduced as my mother and have to be subjected to my friends, who all knew about my reunion and often commented on how much we looked alike and how wonderful it was that we reunited. Even after telling her on many occasions how thrilled I was to finally have her in my life, I felt she still couldn't come to terms with the decision she made almost three decades earlier. This realization was devastating to me because I loved Vanessa so deeply and had hoped that we could have a true mother-daughter relationship.

Liz and I, on the other hand, developed a strong spiritual connection. We behaved like sisters and I could talk to her about anything. I had the connection with Liz that I so desperately wanted with Vanessa. Liz and I would talk by phone long into the night about Vanessa and how sad I was that she was unable to let me in. I told Liz about the incest and my addiction to food and alcohol and she never once blinked an eye. It felt like our souls were inseparable despite the miles that separated us.

Periodically, in the middle of one of our traditional marathon conversations, Liz would lovingly suggest that I try to locate Jeffrey. She felt I had a birthright to know who I was related to by blood. I had to admit that I agreed with her about the birthright part. Still, I insisted I had no interest at all in finding him. I still clung to the fact that he'd been instrumental in the decision to give me away, and since he'd contrived the story about my untimely death, I felt more than just a little bit disgusted with him.

I knew that I had four more aunts out there on Jeffrey's side of the family that I had yet to meet, but that didn't motivate me enough to search for him. I'd never had much concern about my birth aunts, uncles, or cousins. All my life, I'd only wanted my mother, and now I had her, however distantly. With the added pleasure of Elaine, Liz, Adam, Mark, and James in my life, why did I need to rock the boat, throw another stick in my spokes, and try to locate the man who had acted so indifferently about my destiny?

In July of 1996, after much discussion, Liz finally convinced me to try to find Jeffrey. I would be doing myself a disservice, she said, not to seek him out, if for no other reason than to learn whether I had any more siblings and to inform them of my existence. I told myself I made the decision strictly for curiosity's sake. People had often told me I looked most like him and that we shared the same mannerisms. I had to admit I wanted to see the one in the birth family who I so closely resembled.

Liz, always happy to help me out, called directory assistance and asked for a Meredith Babcock. She was

Jeffrey's sister and we knew she lived in Woodland Hills, only minutes from Vanessa and thirty miles from me. Liz told Meredith she was Jeffrey's ex-sister-in-law and wanted his number because she'd been thinking about him lately and was wondering how things had turned out in his life. She never let on that she wanted to track him down to tell him the daughter he'd given up for dead was trying to make contact with him. Meredith reacted lackadaisically. She said she didn't know his whereabouts, but at last contact he'd lived in Madison, Wisconsin. Meredith said she'd look into it and call Liz back with more information.

It was now August, a month later, and we hadn't heard back from Meredith. We decided to call directory assistance in Madison. Liz made the call and asked for a Jeffrey Daniel Sobel III. The operator found only one listing for Sobel in the entire state of Wisconsin! What luck! If we truly had the right man, we had found him far too easily. At that point, I didn't know what to do. All this time I'd pretended indifference, that I really didn't want to find him, and now that I knew where I could reach him, I was too nervous and anxious to make the phone call myself. I had absolutely no reason not to call, no reason not to let my birth father, the one who had given me up for adoption, know all about me. I wanted the man who had announced to the world that I had died to know that I was alive and well and wished to meet him.

I called the phone number a few times and heard on an answering machine the voice of a man who could be in his fifties, perhaps the voice of my birth father. The message relayed no indication that I had the right number, such as "this is the Sobel residence." I listened to the simple message play, hung up, and called back so I could hear it again. Was this my father's voice? I called over and over again, praying no one would pick up, so I could hear his voice in peace.

I didn't feel ready to talk to him yet. Of that I had thoroughly convinced myself. After all, I had never thought of my father while growing up. For some reason, I had thought solely of my birth mother, as if she had become pregnant through an immaculate conception. All those nights I spent lying awake as tears ran hot down my cheeks and I petted the dogs that lay on my bed, the person I longed for, the person I wanted to rescue me, was Vanessa. A father had never entered the picture, perhaps because the relationship I had with my adoptive father had always been much more satisfactory than the one I'd had with my adoptive mother.

On August 13, 1996, Liz came to my rescue when she offered to act as an intermediary and call him for me. All of a sudden, I had absolutely no excuse to say no. I could no longer pretend it all might go away, that I wouldn't have to make the call and open myself up for rejection. She called the home number we'd found and left a purposely casual message on the same machine I'd called repeatedly, hoping it was the right number. The next morning, Jeffrey called her back.

Liz told him she was glad she'd found the right Jeffrey Sobel. He immediately went on guard, curious as to the nature of the call. He knew his ex-sister-in-law hadn't called after all those years just to say hello and shoot the breeze. Finally she came out with it. She told him how she and Elaine had found me a year and a half earlier, and that I wanted him to know I was interested in making contact with him. He became ecstatically happy to hear that I was well. He said he would love to hear from me, and asked Liz to tell me to call him at his office. She told him some rudimentary facts about me, such as my name and that I lived in Glendale, California. She also told him I had brown hair and green eyes, much like him, and I was studying to become a school psychologist. After they had chatted about old times for about twenty minutes, Liz told him that she was going to let me know that he was open to contact.

After she hung up, Liz immediately called me at the temp job I had for the summer. It seemed her voice rang in my ears a bit as she told me we definitely had the right man, that she'd just gotten off the phone with my birth father. My head spun as she told me how excited he was to hear about me, and that he wanted me to call him at his office.

For some reason, I still hesitated to call him, to actually speak with him instead of just listening to his voice on a machine. For one thing, I still ultimately feared rejection, even though Liz had just told me how much it pleased Jeffrey to know that I wanted to talk to him. Secondly, it scared me to think that maybe he wouldn't like me—that unrealistic thought that had invaded my head too often. I told Liz I would call him when I got home and she laughed at my hesitancy.

"Kasey," she said, "we've just found your birth father! He wants to have contact with you. What are you waiting for?"

I felt like a fool for doubting myself, and for thinking I could possibly get through the rest of the workday and accomplish anything with this on my mind.

"If I were in your shoes," she continued, "I would have called him yesterday!"

I hung up and decided to call him immediately.

I searched for a room with as much privacy as I could find, but didn't have much luck. I went into every conference room in search of an empty one, but found that each was either occupied or had a phone that was out of order. I became frantic, almost obsessive. I forgot about my duties as I searched for any semblance of privacy I could find. I didn't care. I would soon talk to my birth father for the first time in twenty-eight years, so who cared about this inconsequential temp job that I hated anyway? I let the phones ring and ring while I found a suitable phone to make the call—the call that would change my life.

I finally located a phone around the corner from my cubicle. It still lacked privacy, but it would have to do. I pressed "9" and dialed the number for Madison,

Wisconsin. It hadn't crossed my mind that my employer would be paying for the phone call.

A man with a deep voice answered the phone.

"This is Jeffrey," he said, a typical office salutation. But this one was different. This time, my birth father had uttered the words. It sent a shiver down my spine.

I talked in a whisper so that no one could hear me. "This is Kasey," I said. Did I need to say I was his daughter?

A brief pause followed, then the calm, soothing voice I'd just heard. "Hello there," he said. "It's so good to finally hear your voice."

I felt an immediate indescribable warmth the moment I heard him say these words. He won me over in that moment, and I believed everything he said. I believed him when he said he had thought about me often over the past twenty-eight years and wondered if I was all right. I believed him when he said he hadn't been able to concentrate on his work since he'd spoken with Liz earlier in the day. And I believed him when he said how happy it made him that I had taken the time to find him.

We talked and laughed and he immediately put me at ease. I felt a powerful, soulful connection with him, just as I had with Liz. This profound connection allowed us to be open with each other from the start. The more we talked the more we discovered that we had much in common. He loved to read and was a wanna-be professional student, as I was. He had a

master's degree in statistics. I would soon obtain my
master's and had worked as a bookkeeper for four
years. We both had a history of substance abuse as well,
and we were both in recovery. We had both lived in
various parts of Los Angeles, and at one point we had
lived within five miles of each other. It struck me that
the world really was a small, small place.

I told him how the other side of my birth family often
said I had his green eyes and thick eyebrows, and how
these facial features had helped me succeed as a child
actress. He asked for pictures of me as a child and I
asked for pictures of him. He told me about his four
other children. He talked about my older half sister,
Michelle, who I already knew about, and added that I
also had two younger brothers, Simon and Dennis, and
a younger sister, Autumn. He told me about his current
marriage, his third, to a woman named Pat, who was in
her early thirties. We spoke of the many synchronicities
in our lives, that my adoptive father was also named
Pat, and that I had a serious boyfriend named Jeffrey
who I wanted to marry three years earlier.

Then he shocked me when he explained why he only
wanted me to call him at work. His wife didn't know
about me! His wife of ten years had no idea that I
existed, and he wasn't ready to tell her. Nobody on his
side of the family knew I existed either. He told me his
entire family still thought that Vanessa had lost me at
birth. He implied he wanted to keep my existence a
secret until he was ready to tell his family.

I could partially understand. After all, the Geigers had sought me out, had found me of their own volition. But I had intruded on Jeffrey's life. He'd never intended to find me, and I had suddenly knocked down his door, so to speak, claiming to be his long-lost daughter.

At the same time, I couldn't believe he'd never told his wife about me. I'd always had the impression that your spouse was your best friend, your soul mate, your confidant—in other words, someone to whom you could tell all your secrets without fear of judgment or rejection. I decided I had no business voicing my sadness over remaining a mystery to so many people, and settled on exchanging phone numbers and addresses with him. He promised he would tell Pat about me now that I'd suddenly come into the picture again.

I hung up the phone and sat back in the office chair. Sounds of the office flooded back over me in an instant, and I felt a little more complete than I had prior to the conversation. All of a sudden, my resentments withdrew to the back of my head, and for that moment, I no longer cared to dwell on the immaturity of a twenty-one-year-old boy who had lied to his family. I wanted to meet him, to look in the face of the man I supposedly took after. I only wanted to know my birth father.

I called Liz immediately and recounted the conversation word for word. I was as high as a kite. My life only continued to get better, and I basked in this revelation. That night, instead of sleeping, I dreamt up one scenario after another in which I would meet my birth father. I thought about what it would feel like to be hugged by him, held by the man who had created me with Vanessa. I wondered about what he looked like now. After all, I hadn't seen any pictures of him more recent than when he was in his twenties. The committee in my head ran a mile a minute, conjuring up fantasies and projections about the new person in my life. Finally, all the pieces of my life that had always remained lost or out of place finally came together. I felt whole. For the first time in my life, I felt like a regular, normal human being, like one who had been born out of love and raised in a traditional family. Thoughts ran through my mind of the Cleavers and families like them, and while I knew I could never regain the childhood I had lost, I had been given a second chance to get to know the people I once thought were lost to me forever.

I went to work the next day tired from lack of sleep but wired with excitement. I found it difficult to concentrate on the menial work of my temp job and continued to think about Jeffrey all morning. I wanted to call him again. I wanted to hear his voice, the voice of the man my birth mother once loved, and know I hadn't made it all up, that I had indeed found my birth father.

However, I was afraid. I didn't want to overwhelm him or become pushy, to inadvertently shove him out of my life. I knew I needed to give him space. It took all I had not to call, to go about my day and pretend I cared about my job. It surprised me when I checked my voice mail in the early afternoon and heard a message from Jeffrey. He said all the things that had gone through my head over the past twenty-four hours—that he couldn't stop thinking about me and wanted to hear my voice again. He said he missed me and was immensely grateful I'd found him.

I called him immediately and told him how much it excited me to know he felt the same way I did. It was during this second conversation of ours that he told me about a spiritual experience he had after our first phone conversation the day before. He described in detail what happened to him as he was leaving his office about an hour after I called him. He said he was walking across the courtyard and suddenly felt my presence, as if he knew exactly what I looked like and who I was in a spiritual sense. He said that he felt an incredible connection to me that could only be described in a poem. He wrote down the poem and sent it to me. It talked about time healing all wounds and the spiritual connection that exists between blood relatives, even when they are separated for one reason or another. Although I believed in the theory of spiritual connection, I was unable to understand his poem. I guess you could say that his theories were over my head. I did notice, however, that he was extremely dyslexic, just like me. We chatted for a while, and when we hung up, I heard him say the three words that I desperately wanted to say myself but was too scared to utter: "I love you."

I listened to these words, and felt an overwhelming sense of peace. For after twenty-eight years, I learned that my birth father loved me. You could only possibly understand what I mean if you are twenty-eight years old and have just heard your birth father tell you for the first time in your life that he loves you. It sounded like music to my ears and resulted in a feeling of pure and unadulterated joy. He loved me. He really loved me. I knew I loved him, just as I knew I loved my mother my entire life long before I ever knew her.

Jeffrey and I set up a system where I could call him at work anytime I wanted to, and he would hang up and call me back so I wouldn't have to pay for the call. After all, I was still a starving student. Since I was instructed to only call him at work, his employer paid for the long-distance calls, many of which lasted over an hour.

The next day, two days after I'd found him, he said that he'd told his oldest sister, my aunt Rebecca, and his wife, Pat, about me. While Rebecca was excited to hear about me, Pat felt quite the opposite. He said he hadn't slept at all the previous night because it had upset Pat immensely. I couldn't blame her. If I found myself in her situation, I would most likely have felt angry and hurt as well. I got the distinct impression that he and Pat already had trouble in their marriage and that the truth about me only added to the stress. He'd already admitted that it scared him to tell her about me because he was hoping she'd forgive him for something else he had done, though he never mentioned what. In other words, revealing the situation with me couldn't possibly have helped matters any.

I worried about his relationship with Pat, and the trouble I might have caused when I suddenly reemerged in his life. I didn't want to create waves in his family. Still, I wanted to know my birth father. He assured me that she would come around and accept me as his daughter, but he didn't convince me. Though I knew little about her, she didn't sound too forgiving by his own description. And despite his assurances, I could tell he probably didn't even believe it himself. I could hear the insecurities in his voice, his fear that things would only get worse between the two of them, that he had indeed stuck himself between a rock and a hard place.

Despite Pat's difficulty in accepting my existence, Jeffrey and I were off and running on a beautiful, fulfilling relationship I hoped would last forever. Suddenly, I wanted to have a relationship with my birth father as much as I wanted one with Vanessa. My giddiness over the idea that I actually had another father easily replaced the indifference I had felt only months before over whether or not to look for him. Jeffrey said it delighted him just as much.

We began to call each other every day, up to five times a day. To my disappointment, I couldn't talk to him on the weekends because he still didn't want me to call him at home. Sometimes Jeffrey would go in to work on Saturday just so he could talk to me. He would call me at seven in the morning and wake me up. He would call just to say hello and we would end up on the phone for hours at a time.

He told me how much he looked forward to meeting me, and filled me in on my half siblings. He told me about his daughter Autumn, who was five years old, and how she cried at bedtime because she wanted to have a sister. Since we were now in contact, he'd told Autumn to pray for a sister. He said he knew I would eventually make her dreams come true. I'd never had a sister, and I wanted one. I wanted to become Autumn's older sister. I knew I would be very good at it. I just knew it.

Michelle, my older half sister, the one he'd had before he met Vanessa, had been adopted by her stepfather. I felt a sting when he told me this, and wondered in that moment if it was a pattern of his to give up his children for adoption. I didn't know I'd been number two to be given away by him. I began to see more and more the immaturity he'd had as a young adult. I wondered how many people give up two children for adoption, and how many would lie about it.

To make matters worse, Jeffrey informed me that after a long estrangement he reunited with Michelle when she reached eighteen, but was no longer in contact with her. He didn't go into detail and I was afraid to ask why, fearing the worst. I tormented myself trying to figure out what had happened between Jeffrey and Michelle. Did Pat not know about Michelle either? Did she forbid him to have contact with Michelle? Did Jeffrey do something that Michelle found unacceptable? What could've possibly happened that would lead to such an estrangement? With all these questions I convinced myself that our case would be different, that there was nothing that anybody could do to separate me from my birth father. There was nothing Jeffrey could do to turn me away from him. After all, the happiness I felt since I'd found him allowed me to gloss over anything he told me, perhaps as a way of protecting myself. The fact that he seemed equally happy to have me in his life made it even easier for me to begin to forget about things that had happened so long ago.

As each day passed we became closer and closer. He said all the right things—everything I always wanted to hear. He had only encouraging and loving words to say. He was quickly becoming another one of my biggest fans, right next to Liz. I talked about my life in great detail but left out the abusive portions, unsure about how he would react to things that I still felt had left me slightly tainted. It touched me that he seemed so interested. My accomplishments made him incredibly proud of me and since I was the only other person in his entire family who was going to have a master's degree, he was glad to know someone had inherited his thirst for knowledge and drive to succeed.

Only weeks after our initial contact, he began to tell

me that Pat still refused to accept me as his daughter. For some reason, she thought I might steal Jeffrey away from her. She was afraid it would upset my three half siblings and suggested that I was after his money and that I wasn't really who I claimed to be. At one point, she actually asked him if we could get a DNA test to prove his paternity. I was infuriated. I couldn't understand how she could think I would lie about something so serious. After all, Jeffrey didn't have millions of dollars and wasn't someone in a position of incredible power. He was just a guy who worked for a living, and I was simply his daughter who wanted to finally be a part of his life.

I had an especially difficult time understanding Pat's anger after I found out she had grown up in foster care and had been adopted herself. I thought she should have found it easier to put herself in my position. Couldn't she imagine what it was like to find your birth father after so many years? One would think that she, of all people, would have a built-in understanding of how important the discovery of my roots had become to me. However, she didn't understand, so again I felt as if I was fighting for my birthright. I began to have the underlying fear that trouble awaited me and I lived in anticipation of the other shoe that would surely drop. I agreed to the DNA testing and Vanessa agreed as well, even though the accusation that I wasn't his daughter angered her. I sent him pictures of me so he could see how much we looked alike, and so Pat could see them and know in an instant that I was his child. I included a letter written purposely with Pat in mind to assure her I didn't want anything but to know my birth father.

I didn't tell her in the letter how often Jeffrey and I had talked on the phone, per his suggestion. Not only had he lied to her by omission about my existence, but he hadn't told her about our multiple daily conversations. I didn't realize this at the time, but Pat was starting to feel betrayed by all the attention he was paying me. I don't know if she ever read the letter, but I know she saw the pictures. Jeffrey told me she thought I was pretty, and she must have seen the resemblance between us because she stopped insisting on the DNA testing, and it never took place. The photographs must have convinced her I was truly his daughter.

Time went on, summer ended, and Labor Day arrived. I'd gone up to Monterey for the weekend and I missed Jeffrey immensely. I convinced myself he would forget about me over the long holiday weekend. I still struggled with thoughts that out of sight meant out of mind. Just from loneliness, I picked up the phone and called his office even though I knew he'd gone out of town as well. At least I could hear the outgoing message on his voice mail—a little reminder that everything was real and had actually happened. I could still easily think it was all just a fantasy. Those emotions still came back every so often.

I checked my own messages periodically, hoping he would call, and he did. He said he'd gotten one of my messages and wanted me to know he thought of me as often as I thought of him. It warmed my heart to know he was out there, hundreds of miles away, thinking of me at the very same moment.

A few days later I got a surprise phone call from Rebecca, his eldest sister, in Omaha, Nebraska. She told me how much it pleased her to hear that she had yet another niece. She mentioned she looked forward to meeting me someday soon. I called her back and left a message of similar sentiment.

I had become obsessed with having Jeffrey in my life and afraid that something would soon happen to change that. I still felt uncomfortable with the way Pat reacted to my existence and the way I couldn't call him at home. I felt the need to cling to every little thing I had that belonged to him, even recordings of his voice on my voice mail. In the beginning, when he would leave a message, I would save it and listen to it over and over again just so I could hear his voice. I even played some of the messages for friends so they would know what I meant when I said how much he loved me and missed me and couldn't wait to meet me. For some reason, I needed validation of his existence and of his love for me, and I held on to these little things with tooth and nail.

In mid-September of 1996, my summer job ended and I began my third year of graduate school, which consisted of a full-time internship. I quickly became unhappy with the school district I was assigned to. The other psychologists there would refer to me solely as "the intern," instead of calling me by my name. They used me as a gofer, a messenger, and a receptionist instead of giving me case studies. I needed to complete twelve hundred hours of fieldwork and had very strict guidelines concerning what kind of training I needed in order to graduate by June of 1997. It soon became apparent to me that I wouldn't receive the training I needed there. To make matters worse, I had to listen to my classmates describe their internship experiences as being fulfilling and exactly what the internship manual stipulated. I knew I needed to find an alternative school district, but I felt stuck. I told myself to hang in there at least a month or two.

I spent most of my time grinding my teeth, just waiting for my next conversation with Jeffrey. I knew he would know just what to say to make me feel better. I used to complain to him about my internship and how they treated me and that I thought about leaving the profession. He would lovingly remind me how smart I was and not to give up—words that I never grew tired of hearing from him. He also reminded me that I don't have to allow anyone to treat me poorly.

Jeffrey and I continued our daily phone calls, and had made plans to perhaps meet at Christmastime. He said he traveled a lot for business, and would arrange to stop by Glendale so that we could meet. I wanted to meet him more than anything, to see my birth father in the flesh. The main thing that kept me going was the fact that I would meet Jeffrey at Christmastime, 1996.

My internship was more bearable with this hope in mind.

My twenty-ninth birthday was quickly approaching and he told me he planned to send me his favorite book as a gift. I could hardly wait to get it, not only because I wanted to know what sort of books he liked to read, but also because for the first time I would receive a gift from my birth father, something I could hold in my hands and know he had also held it in his. The closer it got to my birthday, the more anxious I became to check the mail. The package arrived two weeks late, but I didn't care. I ripped it open with as much exuberance as if I had never opened a present before.

He had sent me *Quantum Healing* by Deepak Chopra, M.D. I had heard about the book and was planning on purchasing it myself. I knew I would enjoy the book immensely, but most importantly, it was the first birthday gift from my birth father and I would treasure it for the rest of my life. I threw aside the wrapping paper like an anxious child on Christmas day. Inside the cover he had written a poem and signed it, "Love overcomes the past. Love Always, Jeffrey Daniel Sobel."

About this time I decided to make a video of myself to send him so he could see what I looked like now, where I lived, who my friends were, and what kind of things I liked to do. I thought I had come up with a rather ingenious and creative way to let him see me the way I am, since I couldn't yet see him in person. I had my friend Frank come to Bernie's house with his video camera and follow me all over the place as I talked to the camera and introduced him to the animals I lived with. He taped me as I went on a hike with my friends and at my twenty-ninth birthday party at my country dance club. We had a blast while we made the tape. All of my friends took turns in front of the camera so they could tell Jeffrey how great I was and how lucky he was to have such a wonderful daughter. I sent the video to his house because he had decided he no longer wanted to keep our relationship a secret. I felt a pleasurable relief. After all, I was his daughter, not his mistress—though perhaps that's how Pat saw our relationship. I didn't see it back then, but she had good reason.

By the beginning of November, I decided to end my internship. My classmates had caseloads of at least ten students, and I had a caseload of one, if I was lucky. I knew I needed to find something better. I stumbled upon another school district that desperately needed a full-time intern—at triple the pay. I interviewed with the staff psychologists and they hired me on the spot. They loved my enthusiasm and told me not to worry about my training, that there would be plenty of work for me to do there. I was ecstatic. I would start work on November 18, 1996. Things were looking up.

Life was great. I knew both of my biological parents and had become confident that I would soon meet

Jeffrey and other members of his family. My salary was about to triple and my new internship had all the responsibility I craved. My life seemed perfect. The future looked bright. My days as a frightened child in an imperfect world had long passed. I had escaped the bonds of my past and had nothing but greatness in my path. What could possibly go wrong?

Chapter 6

Reality Phase

On Sunday afternoon, the 17th of November, 1996, I was relaxing in a hot bath. I had once again contacted my adoptive mother and we were having an unusually pleasant conversation. It excited me to know I would start my new and improved internship the next day and I was telling her all about it. In the middle of our conversation, another call beeped in. In the first second I heard his voice, I knew it was Jeffrey. It pleasantly surprised me to hear from him on a Sunday. After all, we only talked during the week, and occasionally on a Saturday if he went in to work. I told him to hold the line, then told my adoptive mother it was Jeffrey calling long distance so I would have to call her back.

It still excited me every time he called and I wanted to share my happiness over new things as they happened in my life. I noticed almost immediately that he didn't sound like his usual chipper self. Instead, he spoke in a whisper. I could tell he had something serious on his mind, something that was disturbing him. I suddenly felt threatened, uneasy, sure something bad was about to happen. I asked him what was wrong, and my heart sank as he proceeded to tell me the reason for his call.

"Kasey," he said, "I've given this a lot of thought. It hurts me more than you will ever know, but I've decided I cannot continue my relationship with you."

I stopped breathing as his words rang in my ears. I couldn't believe what I had heard. I fully expected he would begin to laugh in a moment and tell me it was all a joke. But he didn't.

He continued, "I need for you not to call me or write to me any longer. It will be easier that way."

"Easier for whom?" I thought. Surely, he couldn't continue with his life as if nothing had happened. Surely he couldn't ignore the fact that the daughter he had given away had come back into his life to give him a second chance. I began to sob uncontrollably. "Why are you doing this?" I pleaded. I couldn't understand how he could do this after we had had such an incredible connection. He replied with very short, truncated answers, as if he'd rehearsed the whole thing and had it scripted out on a notepad in front of him. He refused to give me an explanation. He wouldn't go into detail with me. It turns out that he was unable to talk openly with me because Pat was listening to every word he said. Obviously, Pat had had enough of his paying so much attention to me and was feeling threatened by it. Although I couldn't blame her intellectually for feeling betrayed by him, my heart was breaking. All I wanted was to meet my birth father. As it turned out, I was horribly misguided by a grown man who didn't know how to tell me that he had made a mistake and was afraid to tell me the real reason for cutting me out of his life.

I knew it hurt him to do this, but it killed me beyond words. It felt like the same man had now abandoned me for the second time in my life. The man who gave me up twenty-nine years ago had let me into his life for three wonderful months. As a result, my life had become filled with immeasurable joy and healing. To my dismay he was leaving my life again. I alternated between speechlessness and hysterically yelling at him. I pleaded with him not to let this happen. I begged him not to do this to me and tried to convince him I didn't want anything from him but to love him and my newfound siblings.

It seemed like forever that I stayed on the phone with him as I yelled and screamed, cried and pleaded while he stayed silent on the other end of the line. The whole conversation seemed surreal, like a nightmare, and part of me believed that if I screamed loud enough I would wake myself up from this horrible dream. But as the minutes went by and nothing changed, I began to realize the fruitlessness of my actions.

He remained virtually silent. After all, Pat was right beside him listening and he wouldn't say anything but yes or no. I asked him if he had made this decision of his own accord, and he said yes. He then admitted he had made it only after careful consideration of Pat's feelings. He said he didn't want to lose his family over this, and I thought how bitterly ironic it was for him to say that. God knows I didn't want him to lose his family over the fact that I had entered his life. I didn't see back then that the fact that he was inappropriate with our relationship was what would have caused him to lose his family. It was the five phone calls a day that was unacceptable to Pat. I see now that my presence in and of itself had nothing to do with it. It was the way he reacted to my presence that upset Pat—and rightly so. But back then all I felt was this desperation that he was suddenly erasing me out of his life, never to be thought of again.

I thought it sadly ironic that my entering the picture would threaten his family in any way. Why couldn't he see that my presence in his family would make it more perfectly complete? I only wanted to be one more person to love. Because he loved me didn't mean he had to divide his love more equally among all of us, but only multiply it.

I told him to contact Liz if he ever wanted to find me, because she would always know how to reach me. He said he'd be sure and do that but something in his voice made me feel he never would. I asked him if he'd ever seen the video I'd sent, the one I'd worked so hard to make with all my friends, and he said that Pat had confiscated it before he had a chance to view it. At the time I couldn't understand. How could she not comprehend the bond between us, and that nothing she could ever say or do would change it? I told myself that no matter how betrayed Pat felt, and no matter how long I was locked out of his life, I would still be his daughter and there was nothing anybody could do about it.

I called him every name in the book out of anger, but told him I would never forget him and that I loved him. I also told him I would respect his wishes, even though I didn't want to. He sounded on the verge of tears, and in that second I hated him for not explaining his reasons, which would take me years to understand.

After I hung up the phone, I sat there in shock. I hadn't left the bathtub and the water had turned cold on me. All I could think about was that my birth father was suddenly absent from my life, just like I'd felt Vanessa had become emotionally absent from my life. The feelings of despair were more than I could endure. I wanted both my birth parents in my life and now it felt like I had lost them both. "What am I going to do?" was all I could think, and in the same moment I knew that the answer was "nothing."

I felt utterly, completely alone. For the first time in my life, I honestly understood the meaning of a broken heart. It felt as if mine had been ripped from my chest, twisted about, thrown on the floor, and stepped on with golf shoes. He had broken my heart. He'd lied to me. All those months and all those hours we'd spent on the phone, he'd told me so many times how much he loved me and how much he wanted to meet me and have me in his life. I knew now that it had all been a lie.

I convinced myself that if he really loved me, he wouldn't have let Pat forbid him to have contact with me. But in the end, he himself had made the call. He had made the decision to tell me to stay away and get out of his life. He was a grown man and able to make decisions for himself. I knew I would never let anyone tell me who I could and couldn't have a relationship with. "What a wimp!" I thought to myself. Years now separated him from the immature boy who'd made the first mistake and given me up so indifferently, a sin for which I'd forgiven him a thousand times over. This time it was different. Although a part of me saw this coming, I couldn't get past it so easily.

I became hysterical and began to drive myself crazy with all the thoughts that ran through my head. I couldn't think straight. How could things have gone from so good to so bad in such a short instant? I experienced so many emotions in the minutes that followed the phone call that my mind didn't know which way to turn. I flailed around in the bathtub and got water all over the place as I knocked things over and made a colossal mess of the bathroom. Thank God Bernie wasn't home to witness such self-destructive, self-pitying behavior.

I sobbed, screamed, banged around, and threw things, but nothing helped. I felt like I would never get over the pain. In one fell swoop, he took me back to that place where I felt sorry for myself, and it was a dangerous place to be.

I got out of the bathtub and dried off. I don't know

why, but I called my adoptive mother back. Maybe I did it because we had just spoken on the phone, maybe because in spite of everything, the instinct of every little girl is to call her mother when she feels hurt. I babbled endlessly and ranted in tears about what had just happened. Suddenly my adoptive mother started to cry too. I'll never forget that. All those years I'd felt like she didn't care, yet in the moment I needed her most, she came through for me and seemed truly sorry for my pain.

She didn't understand why he did what he did, and it relieved me to know I hadn't gone crazy after all. I cried and cried and cried and it felt like I would never stop. I stayed on the phone with my adoptive mother because I didn't want to be alone with myself. It's ironic that after all that had happened, in my moment of need I found my adoptive mother's shoulder to cry on, out of everyone else.

After an hour on the phone with my adoptive mother, I finally hung up. Bernie still hadn't come home and I didn't know what to do. I felt as if I'd experienced a death. In a way, I had. Jeffrey would never be there for me again, so he might just as well have died. It would have been much easier to deal with. It served the same purpose. The difference was that he had chosen to leave my life, not that God had decided to separate us. So it seemed much worse than death, really, because I knew his life continued somewhere, miles and miles away. He would move on with his life, for better or for worse, but without me in it.

I experienced pure powerlessness, and because of that I felt hopeless and angry. Nothing I could do would change his mind. He'd made his decision and I had to accept it.

While I waited for Bernie to get home, I called everyone in my phone book. I called Liz and all my friends and cried and yelled and screamed bloody murder. I called everybody but Vanessa. I desperately wanted to tell her what had happened, but deep down I was still afraid to show her my pain. Instead, I called people I hadn't talked to in months. They didn't know what to do with me. After all, none of them had ever experienced that kind of pain. They didn't understand that I wanted the love of my birth father desperately and when I lost it without any explanation, I was distraught. I felt like I was abandoned by yet another family member and I didn't know how much more of this pain I could take. My friends did the only thing they could do—listen to me rant and rave. For that I was truly grateful.

Bernie finally returned and hardly recognized me. He took one look at me and knew I'd had a life-changing experience since the last time we saw each other. I can only remember the way he repeated, "What's wrong, Kasey? My God, what happened?" I told him all about what happened and felt like I had already told the story a thousand times. I still couldn't tell it without bursting into uncontrollable sobs. Bernie felt terrible for me. He hugged me and told me how sorry he felt for me. He asked if I'd expected this, and guessed it probably had to do with Jeffrey's wife.

I didn't get a wink of sleep that night, and the next day I began my new internship. I had eagerly anticipated this day, and now I couldn't wait until it ended. I felt exhausted due to lack of sleep. On one hand, I wanted to be home alone, free to grieve openly for my loss. On the other hand, I felt grateful to have somewhere to go and something to do to keep me occupied. I desperately wanted to keep busy to keep my mind on other things.

It didn't take long before I wanted to call Jeffrey again. I'd become accustomed to his daily phone calls and I missed him terribly. I knew I'd told him I would respect his wishes and not call, but I felt desperate for an explanation, one that he could give honestly without Pat's influence. I needed to know. It drove me crazy not to have closure, and that emptiness gnawed at me and drove me to pick up the phone and dial his number.

I called him at work and got his voice mail. I left a long, sobbing message on his machine and begged for an explanation. I yearned desperately to hear something, anything that would make sense and take away my pain. And truthfully, I wanted him to hear my devastation, to know my pain and understand how much this killed me.

He never called back. He was serious. He really meant to go through with it. This thought staggered me. With each passing day that I didn't hear from

Jeffrey, I sank deeper and deeper into depression. Bernie would find me at home in the dark, clutching the book Jeffrey had given me, my face wet with tears. Bernie had warned me to be careful about Jeffrey when I told him about Pat's reaction to me entering his life. At the time, I'd found his concern touching but ridiculous. How could my birth father possibly hurt me again? I mean, he loved me. He wanted me in his life. He promised to meet me at Christmastime.

I cried at the drop of a hat and nobody could console me. I thought back to my childhood and wondered about the first time I was separated from my birth mother. It may sound strange, but I believe my reaction to being kicked out of Jeffrey's life was similar to how I felt as an infant experiencing the initial abandonment. Nothing anyone could do would take away my pain. I wanted my birth father and I could think of nothing else, much like the way no one could console me as a child when I wanted nothing in the world but my birth mother.

I didn't tell Vanessa what had happened for days. I wanted to tell her sooner, but I feared I'd lose control while on the phone, and I didn't want that to happen. When I finally mustered the courage to call her and let her know what had happened, it shocked her to hear that Jeffrey would let anyone tell him who he could and couldn't have a relationship with. It seemed so unlike the man she'd married so long ago.

I cried and she listened. I felt better after I talked to her and knew in a sense that this second abandonment by my birth father had given Vanessa and me an opportunity to bond—if only for the moment. I told her how happy it made me to have her in my life and that I hoped she felt the same way. Without my asking, she told me that she was not planning on going anywhere. I felt grateful for the reassurance, but it still wasn't enough to ease the pain of losing Jeffrey.

Thanksgiving came a week and a half after our final phone call, and I couldn't stop talking about what had happened, as if the more I talked about it, the more quickly the pain would subside. It didn't.

Christmas came and went and I don't remember much about what I did over the course of the holiday. In general, I just didn't have a good time. I thought about Jeffrey constantly and how he promised me that we would meet. I thought about how he and his family would celebrate the holiday, and wondered if he missed me or regretted his decision. For the most part, I counted the days until New Year's when I could finally put 1996 behind me, at least in physical terms.

In January of 1997, I decided the time had come to move out of Bernie's house. I'd lived there for over a year and he wanted his privacy and his home back. I couldn't blame him. I would have liked to have had the same for myself. It didn't bother me that I had to leave. In fact, it felt somewhat freeing to finally move on. I'd done a lot of nothing since the incident with Jeffrey and now I needed to start making changes. Moving would be just the tip of the iceberg.

I convinced myself it was time for a whole new me. I now made enough money at my new internship to move into my own place and found a nice guest house in Glendale, a place that finally felt like home. I continued to tell myself how independent I was and how I could get past this thing with my birth father, and yet at the same time, I made sure I could keep the same phone number when I moved. I still hoped Jeffrey would call me to tell me he'd changed his mind, that I could still have a place in his life.

I moved to a bigger guest house in June of 1997, was placed on the dean's list, and got my master of science degree in counseling and a school psychology credential. I was eager to be hired as a school psychologist. On June 13th, the educational psychology department held a ceremony for us graduates. I asked Vanessa and Adam to come and they did. Adam drove down from school to attend the ceremony. The next day, my adoptive father and Kimberly threw me a graduation party. Those in attendance were Vanessa, Adam, Elaine, Liz, James, and my friend Sandra. I was so touched that the six-hour drive for Elaine, Liz, and James and the twelve-hour drive for Adam didn't stop them. Our celebration was spectacular and my heart was filled with gratitude. It was one of the best days of my life, and I will never forget it.

Though my adoptive mother and I hadn't spoken since that fateful November afternoon, except to give her my new mailing address, I hoped she would remember my graduation. Still, I heard not one word from her. I kicked myself for thinking she'd remember this time, when I felt she'd let me down so many times before. Every time she forgot something of importance to me, I pulled away from her a little bit more. It surprised me when I went to the mailbox on graduation day and found a card from her. When I saw the return address, I thought to myself, "Wow! She remembered this time!" I excitedly opened the card and read it. To my horror and disappointment, I didn't find a congratulations card at all, but one that read, "Good luck in your new apartment." The card meant nothing to me considering how often I moved. This particular card was no different from the other cards she used to send me. It had food stains on it, and the once snow-white card was now a dull off-white. To top things off, it had a slot to hold a check, but the slot was empty.

I saw myself becoming irate about the money, or lack thereof, and realized something. Through the years I'd felt that since she couldn't tell me she loved me, her financial support was a last-ditch effort on her part to show me some affection. All those years, I'd prostituted myself and treated her nicely. I'd turn the other cheek when she became rude or unfeeling to me, just so that I might profit monetarily in the end. I decided I would no longer allow myself to behave in such a way. I would no longer prostitute myself for her affection, which I never got, or money, which never made me happy in the long run anyway. Then it hit me! My adoptive mother was only able to be there for me when I was hurting. She was there for me when Jeffrey decided to cut off contact with me, but she has never been able to acknowledge the good things in my life. Even when I got a part in a feature film, she was simply unable to be happy for me. She treated that accomplishment and all the others like business-as-usual. Perhaps she was threatened by my success!

Seven months after I had last spoken to my birth father, I felt that I had finally begun to truly move on with my life. The world had opened up before me and I was ready to jump in with both feet. I had remained clean and sober for seven years, two things I would never have thought possible. It was only a matter of time before I would be hired as a school psychologist, my relationship with Liz was growing stronger and stronger, and the achievement of a master's degree nearly made me giddy.

There was only one area of my life that was lacking: a loving and successful relationship. Everything else in my life seemed to be going so well, yet I had been alone for almost four years. I knew that I needed the time to work on myself as I still behaved sophomorically and immaturely in the relationship department. In general, I'd always attracted people in my life who in effect "abandoned" me with their behavior. They did this in many ways such as insulting me, using me, and disrespecting me. It disturbed me to know that I let them do this.

I realize now that I let these things happen. After all, being alone is a much safer place to be, because for me, love ultimately means abandonment of the little girl inside. Until I started to examine my life when I got into recovery, I had unconsciously put myself into situations with men that repeated the pain of my infancy. I entered willingly into unhealthy relationships with emotionally unavailable men so I would experience the absent mother time after time. This behavior became a repetitive cycle in my life, an attempt to heal as I tried again and again, unsuccessfully, to break through the unavailability of all those men. In this way, whenever I found peace in my life, I somehow discovered a way to make it chaotic.

Until Warren Edwards. I met Warren back in 1992 and ever since then had admired him from afar. Tall, dark, and handsome, he commanded attention when he walked into a room. I noticed him the very instant I saw him. He had a successful career and a spirituality that soothed me, the type of man everyone went to for advice about life. He owned his own business and home and was extremely generous. In the past, I

typically avoided men who were successful in so many
areas of their life because I never felt worthy enough to
attract someone spiritually, emotionally, and physically
healthy. As far as I could tell, he stood way out of my
league.

The fact that he smoked cigarettes was the only thing
that disappointed me about him. I'd always told myself
I would never date a smoker. Still, I thought of him
often. I found out later he had also been attracted to me
from that first moment. Alas, we both had other
involvements back in 1992, he in an unhappy marriage
that eventually resulted in a long and painful divorce,
and I in the throes of ending my brief but painful
marriage to Mark.

Over the next five years, Warren and I became
acquaintances. We had the same circle of friends, and
would often run into each other. I always assumed he
didn't have an interest in me. I used to talk about him
to a close mutual friend of ours, and she always told
me how special he was. I assumed he wasn't even an
option. I had never used the word "special" to describe
any of the men who had ever entered my life. I settled
on just admiring him.

The day after my graduation, I ran into Warren at a
party, not unlike many parties where I had previously
run into him. But this time, for some unexplainable
reason, we made our way toward each other and
did something we didn't normally do: we became
engrossed in conversation and talked to each other

exclusively for the entire evening. He became surprisingly yet pleasantly affectionate, which he had never done up to that point, and I didn't know what to make of it. Was something going on here, or was I reading more into this than what was really there? —a typical pattern of mine.

He asked me if I had finished school and he genuinely congratulated me. All this time he'd kept up on my life, because that night he asked me questions about all sorts of things about myself that I had no idea he knew about me. He was concerned about me and interested in my life. I didn't know what I felt, except more than just a little bit of confusion. He threw my mind into a spin when I realized that he had remembered intricate details about my life over the years, something I wasn't used to. How could he remember so much about me, when all this time I thought he didn't really notice me?

It impressed and surprised me that he knew so much about me. He told me he was planning a get-together soon, and asked for my phone number. I gave it to him, expecting this was all purely friendship. Still, I remember that I wrote my number down with an enthusiasm I'd never before experienced when a man asked for my number. I found myself excited and giddy like a high school girl as I wrote the number clumsily on a napkin. I felt so childishly happy that I might as well have written it on his hand in flowery print, a little bubbly heart drawn over the end of the last letter. I watched the exchange from outside of myself and saw myself acting surprisingly playful—in a way I'd never behaved before.

He called less than a week later and we ended up on the phone for three hours. I couldn't believe it. I'd known him for five years, gazing from afar, never able to get up the courage to talk to him for more than a few short sentences, and there we were, unable to get off the phone with one another. We talked about everything from relationships and family to spirituality, education, graduation, traveling, and our careers—basically about the ups and downs of life. Our conversation was real, pure and without all the pretense and egoism I experienced with previous boyfriends. I wasn't just listening to him talk about his life, he was genuinely interested in mine as well.

During our conversation, Warren brought up the topic of my birth father. He had noticed my deep sadness over the last few months and was wondering how I was feeling about it now. We discussed the pain of losing Jeffrey and how seven months had passed since the estrangement.

Up to that point, I knew that many of my friends had grown tired of hearing me rant endlessly on the subject, and I could hardly blame them. I still obsessed and talked about it all the time. But Warren supported me. He listened and assured me it hadn't truly ended and gave me hope that I would someday meet Jeffrey anyway, if I wanted to. He tried to assure me that God still loved me, and if He had plans for me to meet my birth father, then I most certainly would. He added that "God's rejection is your protection," meaning that what may feel now like a huge rejection will eventually, with time, become a blessing. He also told me that some powerful reason must exist if Jeffrey was currently absent from my life and that the reason would become clear to me eventually.

His spiritual certainty comforted me, and I slowly started to believe in what he was saying, because I knew that the story was never over till it's *over*.

It seemed like no time had passed at all before I realized how long I'd been on the phone with Warren. We'd moved on to other topics, such as the difficulty of relationships. I realized I was exhausted, since I'd recently completed my latest move. I knew I needed to hang up and get some rest, but I couldn't find the strength to drag myself away from this man who I now found increasingly fascinating. After a pause, Warren asked me if I would like to go out to dinner with him later that evening. I told him about my exhaustion from moving but that I'd see how I felt later in the day.

I hung up the phone at four p.m. I knew I couldn't meet him that night. I felt far too tired to drag myself out and act social. Instead, I opted to put in a video. I made some popcorn and watched "Mission Impossible" for the second time. When the movie ended at seven-thirty p.m., I remembered that Warren had invited me out for dinner. I stood there looking at the clock for a long moment as I tried to determine if I indeed had time to get ready and go out for the evening. I knew I should stay at home and get some sleep but I felt an energy stirring in me, telling me to get up, get dressed, and go meet Warren. I called him back and asked if he would still like to meet me, and if so, where and when.

Warren was the first person I saw in the restaurant out of forty or fifty people. Our eyes met and he gave me a shy little smile. I shivered inside. I thought he might actually be as glad to see me as I was to see him. In fact, it astounded me to realize how glad I was to see him. I think until that point I'd still felt confused about what exactly had begun to transpire between us, but I knew something would definitely happen soon when I saw him across the room that evening. It seemed like a scene from a movie the way our eyes met like that.

From the moment we sat down, the ease and peace I had experienced with him on the phone earlier in the day returned. One might have thought we wouldn't have had much to say after the hours we'd spent on the phone, but apparently we had lots to talk about. We had a great dinner, drank way too much coffee, and talked until midnight. We were the last ones in the restaurant and the manager finally had to ask us to leave. I didn't want to go home, but knew I had to. I felt caution and exhilaration at the same time. Only months ago, I had still been reeling from the pain of losing Jeffrey. And now, all I'd done was go to a party, a little get-together. Unexpectedly, this fun little ride with Warren had commenced, and I didn't think I wanted to get off quite yet. All I could think of was "don't expect too much." It terrified me to think I might be let down again.

He called the next day as I hoped he would. I came home to find a message from him on my voice mail in which he asked if I wanted to go for a drive to the beach that afternoon. The day was already over by the time I got his message, but I called him back immediately. We talked for another hour and planned to meet that night at his favorite little hole-in-the-wall coffeehouse.

The coffeehouse looked like nothing more than a cozy living room. Though people packed the room, I saw no one but him. As we sat on a little couch in the corner and ate our sandwiches and sipped latte, I really started to examine him. I'd always thought he was good-looking, but I never realized how unbelievably handsome he was until I began to spend time with him. I felt like we had connected in a way I never thought possible. He listened intently as I talked, and because of the way he paid attention, I knew I could tell him anything and trust him, not because I thought he could do something for me later or because I felt I owed him, but because he was honest and open in a way I'd never experienced before.

We sat on the couch and drank coffee until eleven o'clock that night when we went our separate ways. I thought about him all the way home and all the next day. I felt like a girl with a crush. I hoped and prayed that he thought of me, too. My brain had always told me I'm unlovable and that nobody could possibly think of me the way I think of them. I'd always believed in "out of sight, out of mind," just as I'd thought my birth mother was blissfully free of thinking about me or missing me in the way I terribly missed her. As time passed, I came to know that she always thought of me, regardless of the fact that she'd removed me from her life. But this doesn't mean that my thought patterns didn't continue to plague my relationships with everyone I would ever come in contact with, especially Warren.

He called again the following day, and surprised me when he said he couldn't get me out of his mind. He wanted to know if I felt the same way. Amazingly, I told him I did. We ended up on the phone for another hour and arranged to meet the next day. This time, he invited me to his house. I accepted his invitation and began to count the minutes until then.

That evening we spent at his house was one of the most spectacular events, a milestone achievement in my quest to attain a healthy relationship. I made huge strides that night, because that evening I told him all the secrets I never told anyone until they promised in blood not to tell about my imperfections. He already knew that I was adopted, but I told him I was clean and sober for seven years and how Todd had molested me, the big secrets I thought would push him away for good. The same secrets that I waited until I was dating someone a year before divulging. I thought he might laugh at me, like other men had done in the past, but instead he hugged me, an all-encompassing hug that told me he truly cared for me and wasn't going to judge me. He said he'd thought something like that had happened to me. As a child, a comment like that would have proved to me that I was marked as abnormal, unworthy of other human contact. Instead, I saw then his ability to read people and see into their souls, beyond the pain and scarring to the whole person that hid underneath.

For the first time in my life I felt no shame about any of the things I'd hidden inside for so long. I experienced a great relief and was immensely grateful that the shame was gone. My family had always told me never to tell anyone about the horrible things that happened at home behind closed doors. But as an adult and a psychologist, I knew that you were only as sick as your secrets. I believed that secrets will kill you, so I told him everything. We talked for hours and hours.

At the end of the evening, he told me he wanted to kiss me. I leaned toward him and expected fireworks. Instead, I experienced the worst kiss in the world! You can't believe my disappointment. When I look back, I can see I just wasn't in the mood for a kiss. My head still reeled from telling him all my awful secrets. At the time, I thought he was the man of my dreams, yet when the moment of truth finally arose, there wasn't even a spark! We both commented jokingly about it. At least we could laugh over it. He told me later it had worried him that we might have trouble with chemistry, but he would soon throw his doubts out the window. He walked me to my car, and when I looked up at him in the moonlight, I saw this kind man who had heard my most honest confession and hadn't judged me at all, and I kissed him. This time, it was beautiful.

We began to see each other every night. He went to work during the day, and since I was still interviewing for a school psychologist position, I would meet him for lunch and we would talk for a couple of hours in his office. We decided that we were going to take this relationship slowly. I did not want to rush into anything and ruin the relationship like I had done so many times before. I wanted to only hold hands for a while and we did. It felt strange. I only had experience with men who wanted a sexual relationship right away, and if I didn't want that also, they were out the door. But I knew this was different. It became a true courtship, something I'd never experienced.

Two weeks after Warren and I started to date, we spent the day together at the beach, and I can't begin to relate all of the beautiful emotions I experienced that day. Finally, I felt a love that I'd never felt before, the true love I'd waited to experience my entire life. I'd given up on it so long ago that I found myself surprised and pleased to find it slapping me in the face, daring me to deny it. We were just two people who spent the day together on the sand and surf, but to me, it felt like the beginning of a new chapter in my life, one where I could share myself with another human being and not feel in debt to them or in constant fear of them leaving me.

He'd told me he had made a tape of all the songs that made him think of me, and as we drove to the beach that day, he played the tape for me. I was so touched when the first song began to play and it was my all-time favorite country love song, "I Cross My Heart" by George Strait. We both sang off-key at the top of our lungs and it instantly became our love song. I couldn't get over the fact that of all the songs in the world, he'd picked that particular one as his favorite.

At the beach, we bought fresh fruit and fed it to each other. We acted playful and flirtatious and the day continued to get better and better. It seemed like pure heaven. When we finally made it home, as the sun set behind us into the California surf, we stood in the kitchen and shared strawberries, our lips passing the sweet fruit from one mouth to the other, tasting the moist sweet sensation simultaneously. At that moment, I knew I loved him, that we shared a passion like I'd never experienced before.

All day, our physical contact had stopped at holding hands. I'd never fallen in love from holding hands before. I thought I'd fallen in love when I had sex, and when I forced other men to prove to me that they cared about me. I thought I'd fallen in love when someone seemed perfect, after I examined them for hours on end for flaws and imperfections. In truth, I'd always been pretty stuck-up. I had a three-page-long mental list of impossible criteria men had to meet before I would give them the time of day. This way, things stayed uncomplicated for me. I could easily avoid attachments on the basis of their failure to meet my specified criteria. Warren and I were developing a simpler relationship. My interaction with him flowed and I knew he cared about me more than anyone ever had in the past. I let him into my soul and he responded with respect and admiration. I couldn't believe my good fortune.

That night, we went to a friend's house together, the first time we went to a group function as a couple. Throughout the course of the evening, we hung out with our friends and we would periodically check in with each other. Suddenly, for the first time in five years, I saw something in him I didn't like. Thinking back, I can't even remember the remark, but I do remember that I overheard him bantering about life with one of our friends. I didn't realize they were just kidding with each other. All I remember is that I saw a very cynical side of Warren, and I didn't like witnessing that in him. Forget the fact that I am as cynical as the next person.

I know this sounds silly, but my heart and my mind conflicted. I saw a side of him that disturbed me, but I had already become hooked on him. In addition to all the wonderful qualities, I saw before me a very cynical man. Of course, my mind flew to the worse-case scenario. I convinced myself that instead of the wonderful man I'd grown to love, he was only a cynical, crass man. Mind you, I based this solely on one comment I overheard him say to a friend who no doubt had a long history with him. But that's how my mind works. I overreact, think the worst, and make it happen. Unfortunately, I had fallen in love with him. How could I just turn off the feelings that stirred in me? I became instantly afraid and began to deny all the positive qualities in him. It didn't take him long to figure out what was wrong. He sensed my dilemma and we talked about it.

People I knew in successful long-term relationships had always told me that nobody is perfect, and that if you love someone they have the capability more than anyone else in the world to make you angry. Now I understood both these sentiments. I also understood the other thing they'd told me: that the one you love will bring more joy and celebration into your life as well.

I knew that perfection didn't really exist, but for some reason I had come to believe that he was perfect. I remember how we sat on his couch later that evening and talked about the incident. He attempted to explain to me that he and his friend had always had this relationship—that they were very cynical with one another in fun. He assured me he was joking, and told me that we both needed to accept each other for the way we are. He told me I was the best thing that ever happened to him, and he would regret it if I left over such a petty issue. I knew in my heart he was right. I knew beyond a shadow of a doubt that he was the best thing to happen to me as well. Thankfully, he knew my entire history. He knew I was a runner and he called me on it. I knew I would make a mistake if I broke this thing off before it even got started, but that was my cycle. In truth, the intimacy developing between the two of us terrified me to death.

When I got home that night I could barely sleep at all. I awoke once in tears, completely confused as to what exactly had happened over the course of the evening. My mind raced about what I should do. The judgmental voices went into a heated battle. One said I blew it. Another berated me for my simple-mindedness, and still another accused me of behaving just like my adoptive mother. After all, I felt like I had to be perfect, too. I allowed my adoptive mother's voice to rise above the others, and as I heard all the cruel and judgmental things she always said, sleep deprivation allowed me to believe them.

I called a friend the next morning in tears. She didn't know what to do with me. She wasn't adopted and couldn't possibly understand all the facets that were involved in a simple relationship for me. Basically, she didn't understand what the hell I was talking about.

"What do you mean he treats you so well you can't stand it?" she asked. "So what if he isn't perfect? Get over yourself, and move on!"

I thought for sure that the relationship between Warren and me had ended. I'd made him feel bad when I judged him for something I viewed as an enormous character flaw, and I'd successfully made myself feel like a degenerate loser. Behavior like this becomes a self-fulfilling prophecy. You allow yourself to get into a mind-set that you aren't lovable, and when true love finally comes along, you don't know what to do. That's the way it felt for me.

I debated over whether I should call him. I spent hours unable to convince myself one way or the other. Thankfully, he called me. We talked at length and I apologized for being so grossly judgmental and critical of him. I tried to explain how I tend to blow everything out of proportion and that I was acting like an infant. I knew I had to grow up. He apologized for his own behavior—though he didn't need to—and my respect for him grew that much more. Our dating resumed and we continued to see each other every night until the end of the summer. And every night, when I left his house to go home, he would ask me to call him to let him know I'd arrived safely. I'd get home after a fifteen-minute drive, call him up, and we'd stay on the phone for two hours. I couldn't believe how much I enjoyed our relationship, and my love for him deepened with each day that passed. I began to accept him more, and he extended the same acceptance toward me. Finally, it seemed, the last piece in the puzzle of my existence had fallen into place.

The wheels of my life had begun to spin, and the end seemed nowhere in sight. Finally, I felt like I had begun to live the life of a normal adult human being. After a long string of interviews, a large school district in southern California hired me as a school psychologist. Before the school year started, though, Warren and I closed out the summer by taking a six-day trip. Of course, the trip wouldn't have been complete without at least one practical joke by Warren.

Prior to the trip, he had told me over and over how he would take me to his favorite romantic spot and spare no expense in the process. With this in mind, I eagerly awaited his plan. I loved surprises, and I couldn't wait to see what place Warren found romantic. I was curious to see if I agreed with him. He had good taste in the finer things in life, so I knew I was in for a great treat. He didn't tell me much about the intricacies of his plans, only that our destination was a popular coastal town.

When we turned off the freeway, butterflies churned in my stomach. I looked around at the beautiful view and thought, "So far, so good." As we drove along the coast, my eyes curiously perused the long line of majestic hotels and quaint restaurants. Any of them would have suited me just fine. All of a sudden, Warren pulled into the most dilapidated motel on the strip. The outer walls looked especially dirty in the bright sunlight, and a vacancy sign flashed in bright neon.

"Oh, good!" Warren exclaimed. "There's still a vacancy!"

He parked the car, and I kept my mouth shut. I looked around the parking lot while he checked a map.

I noticed on the crooked marquee the highlight of staying at this motel—they offered HBO. They had conveniently placed the ice machine right next to the rooms, and you parked right at your doorstep. I thought about what he'd repeated all week—a romantic getaway, no expense spared. Another flashing light interrupted my thoughts. It read "$20.95 a night."

I took a deep breath and reminded myself that I trusted him. I told myself this place must be some hidden treasure, that maybe it looked a little rough around the edges, but housed the coziest rooms along the entire coast. Miraculously, I believed in my heart that I would go anywhere, stay anywhere, and do anything with this man, so if this was his favorite hideaway, it must be special. This time, Warren interrupted my mental conversation.

He started the car and said, "Since we found the motel, why don't we check out the restaurants so you can choose which one you'd like to go to?"

I smiled and said okay. As we drove, Warren told me how much I would love the motel. By this time, I had the idea that he had something up his sleeve. I couldn't wait to see it. I assured him I looked forward to experiencing the inside of the room. As I said it, he turned the car into the driveway of the most beautiful high-rise hotel in town. He parked the car, and as we got out, he told me they had a great restaurant inside that we could go to. I smiled, thinking I'd figured things out. Obviously, he had saved his money for fancy meals!

With a Cheshire-cat grin on his face, he directed me into the lobby of this beautiful hotel and walked up to the counter. He pretended to inquire about the restaurant and then, under his breath, gave the hotel attendant his last name and reservation number. As I observed this, I realized he had reserved a room at this hotel. It turned out to be a majestic suite on the top floor where all you could see from the balcony was pure Pacific Ocean. I'll never forget the first moment we entered the suite, when I set my suitcase down and looked up to find a beautiful bouquet of flowers sitting on the table. Warren had sent them, of course, "just because." I couldn't believe it. Warren had pulled the practical joke to end all practical jokes. And I fell for it —hook, line, and sinker.

We came back from our week of breathtaking sunsets, walks on the beach, massages, swimming, and fancy meals, with feelings of new love. I started my job with the school district the following Tuesday, and it pleased me to find that I loved the field of school psychology as much as I had anticipated. What a thrill to get paid to do something I love!

I turned thirty in October of 1997, and Warren threw me a birthday party. Little by little, birthdays had become easier and easier to tolerate as I healed and assimilated into my new life with my birth family. While I was sitting with my friends at the party laughing and having a good time, a rooster walked in —a bigger-than-life walking, talking rooster! As if this in itself wasn't amazing enough, this "rooster" knew my entire life story. He sang out a lyrical rhyme about everything I'd ever done, from childhood stories about me on location with actors I'd worked with to anecdotal tales of my later life. We all laughed and I couldn't wipe the smile off my face because I knew that Warren had something to do with this. It turned out this was no ordinary rooster, because this one could lay eggs. After he laid an egg in front of the guests, he instructed me to open the biggest and brightest egg in the nest. Inside I discovered a banner that read, "Happy 30th Birthday, Kasey! Love, Liz, Elaine, Adam, James, Vanessa, and Mark."

As it turned out, Warren had secretly communicated with my birth family so they could arrange the unforgettable this-is-your-life performance. I enjoyed that birthday immensely. In fact, my birthdays were getting easier and easier each year. It certainly helped to dampen the ever present depression that always arose on that day, regardless of how good things were going in my life. Basking in my wonderful birthday celebration, I knew that many people loved me. About that, I finally had no doubt. I knew that Warren loved me beyond description and that I felt just as strongly toward him. I knew that I was here to stay.

In December of that year, Vanessa turned fifty. Warren and I drove to Monterey where Vanessa, who drove there separately, and the whole family gathered for a birthday party dinner. We took her to a concert of one of her favorite performers, which she enjoyed immensely. Vanessa didn't know I was coming, so I planned on being the big surprise of the party. She seemed glad to see me, but we didn't get much of a chance to talk or spend time together. Since Vanessa and I didn't keep in close contact with each other, even though we lived only thirty minutes apart, I was disappointed to say the least. I hoped that this would be a good opportunity to spend some quality time together.

For the first time in the three years I'd known her, I realized how close she was to her son, my brother Adam, and noticed that she focused all her attention on him during the weekend. It felt like she avoided contact with me and smothered him throughout the entire weekend. Once again, all my insecurities flooded back in a torrential attack. I felt myself reverting to old feelings, and saw myself briefly as the outsider again as I watched a mother with her son and jealously wished I was as close to her as he. In an instant, I remembered all those times I'd spent growing up, the times I'd prayed that someday my birth mother would come to take me away from the loneliness I endured in her absence. Intellectually, I understood her connection with Adam. After all, she'd raised him since birth. But emotionally it crushed me. I wanted her to be a mother to me, and all I saw was Adam getting too much mothering. I started to wonder if she really saw me as her daughter, or just as a constant reminder of a painful part of her life. I knew in that moment I hadn't accepted the fact that she didn't raise me. I wanted her to have raised me. I wanted her to connect with me as she did with Adam.

Also in December, my adoptive mother made plans to move to South Carolina where Peter now lived. A part of me was pleased that she'd be somewhat absent from my life. I felt that the distance between us would do us some good. She asked me to help her with a garage sale she wanted to have in preparation for the move, and she also asked whether I could take her to the airport if she arranged a flight on a weekend. Since I wanted to be the good daughter, I obliged. I arrived at seven a.m. for the garage sale, and dutifully manned the backyard. She made a special point of showing me where she'd hidden a valuable pair of antique sunglasses, and I was determined to keep a watchful eye on them. I showed them to only one customer who had expressed a mild interest, but he opted not to purchase them. I immediately put the glasses back in their secret place.

My adoptive mother phoned the next day and tearfully told me that someone had stolen the sunglasses. I recognized in her tone of voice an insinuation that I'd been lax in my duties. I knew that tone only too well. In all honesty, she never came right out and made an accusation. She never said, "It's all your fault." Instead she said, "I told you to be careful with those sunglasses. I think I know who stole them.

Do you remember the man who spent a good two hours there searching through everything?" I said yes, all the while knowing that I kept a very close eye on those sunglasses, and if they were missing, it wasn't because of anything I had done. I told her that only one man, the same person she was referring to, asked to see the sunglasses the entire day.

Once again, I allowed her to make me feel guilty for something when I hadn't done anything wrong. I told her exactly where I'd put the glasses after the customer left, and she insisted she'd checked but absolutely couldn't find them. She told me how devastated she was since the glasses had belonged to her mother, my grandmother Elizabeth, and said she must be rolling over in her grave now because of this mishap. I bit my tongue, wanting to say that if they were that damned important, she never should have put them in the garage sale in the first place.

I felt horrible. I knew my adoptive mother couldn't "send me back" to the adoption agency like I'd always feared as a child, but I still felt I had failed her once again. In my heart, I knew the glasses were still there because I made sure no one was looking before I put them back in the cupboard, but because she was my mother, I felt I had to trust her. I began to berate myself once again for screwing up.

She called again the next day elated. "Guess what!" she said. "I found the glasses. They were right where you said they were!" Instead of being happy she'd found them, I became furious with her. I'd known they were there all along, but she'd refused to listen to me.

Finally, something switched off in me. I had finally had enough of her manipulations. I had finally had enough of listening to her attempts to blame me for her divorce from my adoptive father. I was tired of her ignoring my accomplishments and putting me down. For the first time in my life, I realized that I no longer had to be the perfect daughter. I no longer had to allow her to treat me like an extension of her right leg. I could say no to her. I could disagree with her.

I was no longer willing to treat her with respect when I felt she would treat me poorly in return. Warren had repeatedly called me on this pattern of mine. He helped me realize I don't need to have people in my life who bring me down or are abusive to me, even if it is my adoptive mother. For some reason, when Warren said it, it finally clicked.

The straw that broke the camel's back was when she mentioned that she changed her flight from a Saturday, when I didn't have to work, to a weekday, when I would have to take most of the day off. I knew I was simply unwilling to do this for her. It's sad, but that's how I felt. When I attempted to discuss my feelings with her, she refused to listen and hung up the phone.

Sadly, I didn't hear from her again. I later heard from my adoptive father that Todd decided to move to South Carolina with her, and since he's afraid to fly, they drove cross-country together. All that heartache for nothing! As far as I know, she left for South Carolina the third week of December, 1997.

M y troubles had shifted from one mother to another within a week. At Christmastime, I found myself reminded again of the emotional distance that remained between Vanessa and me. It hit me harder than I expected. On our fourth holiday together, I drove to Liz and James's house. I arrived at noon the day after Christmas as planned with my bags filled with gifts for everyone. I expected the usual family crowd: Vanessa, Adam, Liz, James, and Elaine. Instead, I walked in to find Liz, James, and Elaine in the living room with strangers.

Vanessa was nowhere to be found. It turned out that she'd left five minutes before I arrived because she suddenly found out her job might be in jeopardy. Upset, she left for L.A. taking Adam with her. It devastated me to find her gone. I had difficulty understanding why she left without waiting to see me. I felt numb. I had to act polite and smile and pretend that everything was okay as Liz introduced me around, but inside I was dying.

Liz introduced the strangers as James's daughter Jessica, her husband, and their two young adopted daughters. I liked them immediately and felt a bond between myself and the young girls. I didn't tell them I was adopted, but I felt an immediate connection with them and wondered if they felt unhappy during the holidays the way I had as a child. The three of us hung out together all day. They helped me move beyond the initial disappointment I'd encountered upon missing Vanessa.

Six hours later, Vanessa called to let everyone know that she and Adam had made it home okay. I heard Liz talking with her on the phone, and waited eagerly. I fully expected Vanessa to ask to speak with me. She didn't. In fact, I overheard Liz asking her if she wanted to speak with me and she said no. At that very moment, I knew that Vanessa didn't think of me as her daughter. I suppose deep down I knew that she was emotionally incapable of letting me into her life, but now it felt final. My disappointment was almost unbearable. She'd left a gift for me, and I held back the tears as I opened it. I was crushed.

I excused myself and found a phone in the back room to call Warren. I felt foolish but I was hysterical. I felt like I had lost both mothers within two weeks. I felt I had lost my adoptive mother when she cut off contact with me and moved out of state, and after three years of reunion I had to let go of my dreams of having an intimate relationship with Vanessa. I had to accept the fact that she didn't see me as her daughter. I had to accept the fact that she didn't feel about me the way I felt about her. I wanted to share my life and all its ups and downs with her, but she didn't seem to want that. I realized that I still considered our holidays together to be a special event. Perhaps she didn't. Warren assured me it was all right to feel sad, and to love her anyway. I expressed to him my utter devastation, and while he didn't quite know what to say to me, he expressed his genuine concern. Mostly he just listened like he always did and his attention had a calming effect on me. He reminded me that I could enjoy my time there with the others or come home if I wanted to.

His advice brightened me a bit. I decided I wouldn't let this little emotional setback ruin the great time I could have with the rest of my birth family. I finished up my phone call with Warren and went back to the party. I spent the rest of the evening immersed in conversation and played games with James's young granddaughters. When I came home I went directly to Warren's house and we resolved to spend the next Christmas out of town.

Chapter 7

Growing Up

Nineteen ninety-eight proved to be a year full of learning, especially in the arena of relationships. Oftentimes, Warren needed to work long hours, and when he got home from work, he was often tired, preoccupied, and not quite himself. I missed him horribly when he wasn't able to call me as often as usual. During these times, my fears that he would forget about me, though ridiculous, were in full force. He'd spoiled me by treating me so well, so the loss of his attention when he had to stay at work late only heightened my feelings of abandonment. I began to believe this was some sort of test to prove to me that "out of sight" didn't necessarily mean "out of mind."

Whenever Warren worked late, he called me every night after he got home, no matter how exhausted he felt, if only to talk to me for thirty seconds to let me know he was thinking about me. I had to make a concerted effort not to call him at work as often as I normally would because I knew he had millions of things to do and I didn't want to distract him. It was hard because I had a strong desire to talk to him every day, just to say hello and tell him that I love him.

Although my relationship with Warren continued to go well, thoughts of Jeffrey began to haunt me again. I knew he had reasons for leaving my life. What was my problem? Why wasn't I over it yet? I became very moody, and during my weekend visits at Warren's house, he would sometimes find me in the bathtub in hysterics. At other times, I would uncontrollably burst into tears in the middle of a meal. Perhaps my shallow relationship with Vanessa added to my inability to let go. I was in a wonderful relationship sharing my life with a man I truly loved, yet I felt unhappy enough to burst into tears all the time. I thought over and over about the way Jeffrey had told me he didn't want me in his life any longer. Though I wanted to forget about it all in the worst way, my mind seemed drawn to his memory, and my fear of abandonment soon became overwhelming.

Since Warren was the closest one to me at the time, I managed to transfer all those negative emotions from thoughts of Jeffrey onto Warren. I became afraid he would leave me or trade me in for someone else. Because of this fear, I became suspicious and overly critical of everything he did. I began to count the number of times he told me he loved me. If he didn't tell me at least once a day, I became convinced he had fallen out of love with me.

It amazed me how quickly those feelings became stronger than the reality of how kind, sweet, and gentle he was to me. The fact that he was a perfect gentleman became overshadowed. I forgot about how he would open the door for me and order for me in restaurants after I told him what I wanted. He'd say to the waiter, "The lady will have . . ." I loved that. Nobody ever treated me like that before. My ex-husband treated me horribly and ex-boyfriends either insulted me or complained about my weight, suggesting I could lose ten pounds, as my adoptive mother had done.

All of a sudden, I realized what the problem was. I knew that my relationship with Warren was the real thing—and it scared me to death. I couldn't understand how I could possibly feel threatened with a man who loved me, treated me with respect, and possessed all the traits I'd ever wanted in a man. Clearly, we had true love the way it should be—pure companionship coupled with intimacy and friendship. For most of my life, I'd looked for the Hollywood version of true love, the one I'd seen played out in one box-office hit after another, full of raw sex, repeated I-love-you's, and phone calls five times a day.

I knew I needed help. I could feel myself starting to sabotage the relationship the way I'd sabotaged every good thing in my life. I began to test him daily. I felt trespassed against all the time. He would make some innocuous statement like, "Did you know you have a stain on the front of your blouse?" and I'd blow it completely out of proportion and take it as some sort of ultimate insult on my soul. I asked him repeatedly if he loved me. His actions screamed out his love for me, but it was somehow never good enough. He could never possibly hold me tight enough or long enough.

Inevitably, we reached a point in our relationship when the phone calls and the time we spent together diminished—after all, we both had full lives. As we relaxed into our relationship, our true colors began to emerge. In my mind, I knew we had a normal and healthy relationship, but I wanted to run again. In the past, whenever things had gotten uncomfortable or confusing, my answer had always been to run. But this time, I felt determined to see it through.

It scared me to show Warren my real self, bad points and all. I felt I had to be perfect or I would lose him, just as I had always felt I'd lost my mother because I wasn't the perfect baby. Well, finally I'd found the man that all those love songs talked about, and I became bound and determined not to blow it this time. I refused to let something that happened thirty years ago ruin my life. Still, as our relationship progressed, my fears worsened. The more in love we fell, the more afraid I became. It seemed I constantly waited for the other shoe to drop and nothing could convince me it wouldn't.

I wasn't the only one who learned from the growing pains of our relationship. We had to work on opposing traits and meet somewhere in the middle. I wavered between clinging and pushing him away. I needed to learn to lighten up on my need for affection and the desire for him to hold me. No one can hold hands twenty-four hours a day! He, on the other hand, needed to let me in and be more demonstrative.

One problem remained. In truth, he could tell me he loved me a hundred times a day and still fall one short of making me happy. For me, nothing was ever enough. When I felt good about myself, hearing someone say "I love you" became less and less important. But when I felt bad about a situation I became a needy, inconsolable infant, precisely as I must have felt at three months of age when I longed for the touch of my birth mother. In short, it was as if I was dealing with and grieving the loss of my birth parents all over again. When I reached that place, the tears became gut-wrenching and came from the deepest part of my soul. And when the tears came, even the man of my dreams, the one who treated me like a queen and like the best thing that's ever happened to him, couldn't quiet my sadness.

When I felt upset, I isolated. Deep down inside, I only wanted someone to hold me and listen to me, but the closeness and intimacy was sometimes unbearable. The physical proximity of intimacy was even excruciating at times.

Honesty scared me to death. If I let you into my life, I was sure you would see the truth of who I was and you'd be forced to run, and if you didn't run, I most certainly would. And often, I wondered why anyone would bother to try and get close to me. Who would want to deal with an orphan who couldn't bond with her mother and who therefore tried her damnedest not to bond with you? I've always wanted the passion, excitement, and attention that comes with the initial dating process, when everything is new and it seems neither of you will ever run out of things to say to one another. But as soon as the "ho-hum" stage arose and he didn't call me as much as I'd like or send flowers anymore, I was ready to take off.

It scared me to find myself in such unhappy times when things on the surface were going so well. I decided to reenter therapy for the umpteenth time and tell my story yet again. I knew I should have gone back to therapy the day Jeffrey cut off contact with me, but for some reason I wasn't ready—perhaps I was afraid to look at the harsh reality of the situation. Luckily, I found a wonderful, supportive therapist and I proceeded to tell him the whole sordid story about Jeffrey and went through many tissues while trying to get through it. Unfortunately, my therapist lacked training in dealing with issues of the adopted. At times I felt like I was explaining the issues to him, so that he could in turn help me sort them out. I tried in vain to explain my fear of abandonment and the horrors that consumed me when I would lie awake late at night thinking of how I would eventually come home to an empty house and a note from Warren that would read, "I love you, but I have to leave." The therapist listened intently, like all my friends and the rest of my support network, but it still wasn't enough.

I wanted someone I could go to who knew the answers of the universe, so I had unrealistically high expectations of my therapist. When I tried to explain to him that I became devastated if I suggested we go to a movie and Warren didn't want to go, he didn't know what to say to me. He'd say, "There's no easy answer," but I thought there must be, if only I could ask the right questions of the right person. In the meantime, it crushed me when Warren responded in such a way. It seemed impossible that I could think like an adult and realize that a million other reasons might make him not want to go to a movie—maybe he was tired, maybe he preferred to do something else, maybe he had a headache. Instead, I assumed he didn't want to spend time with me. I constantly waited for the other shoe to drop. Warren showed the appropriate concern. He'd ask when I would have my next therapy session, and I'd tell him, though I knew it would help little to alleviate the pain.

I'd told myself for years that I needed to join a support group for adoptees—or start a support group if nothing like that existed. I knew that others who had experienced similar situations would understand my insecurities regarding relationships. Although my need for support was constant, I always denied its existence —perhaps because I once again felt all alone, as if I were the only one in the world who had difficulty in reunion. After all, I kept reading these stories of happily-ever-after reunions in which birth mother and child were best friends and perhaps even lived together. Looking back, I am amazed that I was so ignorant about this. I was very perceptive and aware of resources that would help my students and their families, but I was blind when it came to finding support for myself.

When the pain got to be too great and a few friends and colleagues suggested I seek out a support group, I decided to do some research on the Internet. After a little searching, I discovered a plethora of resources and support groups to choose from. I couldn't believe it. There was plenty of support out there just waiting for me to access it. Finally, in February of 1998 I went to a Concerned United Birthparents meeting that was only fifteen minutes from my home. This was a support group that welcomes all members of the triad (birth parents, adoptees, and adoptive parents). I felt very nervous. Even though I knew intellectually that someone there had experienced everything I had, the perpetually agonizing committee in my mind told me I was still different from everyone there, and that I had deeper and darker secrets.

At the meeting, they handed out colored poker chips. Red meant you had a burning desire to share something with the group, and blue meant you felt you had nothing you needed to discuss. I jumped up and grabbed a red chip. I knew immediately that I needed to speak up and be heard. I knew from experience that if I didn't open up and talk about the things that bothered me, they would eat me up inside. With this in mind, I stood up and shared first. I told a group of thirty strangers the horrible story of how my birth father had cut me out of his life. For the first time, I saw in the eyes of others a look of compassion and empathy. These people had been there, and they subtly but clearly let me know it. Even the birth parents present understood to a degree.

When the meeting ended, I wandered over to a table filled with literature on adoption and resources to help one deal with the pain surrounding adoption. I sifted through the books and pamphlets in search of answers, and found a flyer for a meeting that had just started up for adoptees only. They called themselves Eetpoda, which spells "adoptee" backwards. Finally, a solution! It sounded exactly like the group I needed, and the next meeting was only a week away at a location less than an hour from my home.

I decided it was more than worth it to drive the distance. I convinced myself I would find Eetpoda full of people who would understand me and know what to do with me—God knows I had no idea what to do with myself. So the next Saturday, I drove forty-five minutes away, in search of yet another answer.

I cried throughout the entire meeting. Everyone told stories—the ones who had had happy homes and the ones who hadn't—and in everything they said, I heard a little bit of my own life. I was quite relieved to hear that while my adoptive home was the exception, my feelings and reactions to my situation were typical. I was amazed to hear the stories of adoptees who had been raised in loving homes with no abuse or foster care experience, yet still had great pain in their lives. No wonder I was in pain. Not only was I dealing with the loss of my birth family as a child, but I was also dealing with the added trauma of sexual abuse and an unpleasant relationship with my adoptive mother as a child, and the sudden estrangement from my adoptive mother and my birth father as an adult.

Our feelings became the common denominator between us. Everyone there—regardless of what story they had to tell or the silence they chose to maintain—had felt different, worthless, lonely, and afraid that their loved ones, husbands, wives, and significant others would leave them. I saw this common thread running through our relationships, and was relieved that others felt as I did. Attending these meetings introduced me to great friends and allowed me to work on the acceptance of where I fit into my adoptive mother's and Vanessa's life. I didn't like the lack of depth in my relationship with them, but I wanted to accept and love them anyway.

I explained to the group that the man in my life loved me perfectly, yet I still felt the need to test his love to make sure. I told them that when he made me breakfast in the morning, I would sometimes say, "You don't have to make me breakfast if you don't want to. Don't go to any trouble." "Of course I want to," he would inevitably say, because he loved to make me breakfast. And if he didn't tell me he loved me, I became sure that he must be involved in an affair or just didn't care anymore. I recounted in detail to them how I sometimes provoked the very rejection I feared. I used to tell Warren that I was not going to be affectionate toward him anymore because it was obvious that he had no desire to reciprocate. Needless to say, Warren has never given me any indication that he has "lost that loving feeling." It has always been in my head. As I gave the group countless examples of my insecurities, they nodded and some even cried along with me. They understood what is was like to fear being abandoned by the ones you love, yet behaving in such a way as to make it impossible for them to stick around. I knew my thoughts bordered on insanity, but those adoptees understood.

It was at this first meeting that they suggested I read some books on adoption and its aftermath. They assured me that there were many books available that would help me process my adoption issues and reunion difficulties in relation to both my birth and adoptive families. I took their advice and read book after book on the subject, each time seeing myself described in the pages before me. If I read a book that was particularly helpful to me, I asked Warren to read it so that he could gain some perspective on why I behaved the way I did. It was an extremely helpful process—for me because I finally felt validated, not crazy, for having the feelings I had, and for Warren because he had felt so helpless and now had strategies on what to say to me and how to deal with me when I was in pain.

Ever since that first time I attended a support group meeting, I have talked to many adoptees so that through them I might better understand myself. After all, they understood me like no one else ever had before. They laughed, and helped me to laugh too, at the insanity of our collective insecurities. I also continued to talk to other members of the adoption triad. I would discuss with adoptive parents the nature of the relationship I had with my adoptive mother and they would help me put everything in perspective. They knew like no others what it is like to raise an adopted child and the challenges it affords. They helped me to see what my adoptive mother was dealing with in her own life that may have led her to treat me the way she did. Each time I spoke with an adoptive mother who was loving and gave her adopted child wings with which to fly, I was able to see that my adoptive mother just didn't have the ability to adequately show me she loved me the way I needed to be loved.

Likewise, I would talk to birth mothers who were also in reunion and they would tell me that Vanessa is operating on paralyzing fear. Fear that they too had experienced until they dealt with it. They would assure me that Vanessa loves me very much, but to actually express her feelings would be far too painful for her. Every time I talked to a birth mother who had dealt with her guilt and shame around the relinquishment and was able to tell the world that she has a child she gave up for adoption, I had hopes that one day my birth mother would be able to move past her pain and do the same.

All in all, by reaching out to others, I discovered that my situation was not all that unusual. I learned that adopted children often have strained relationships with their adoptive mothers, and that birth mothers often have a difficult time getting over the guilt and shame of giving up a child. I also learned that the situation with my birth father was typical. Significant others often have a hard time with the long-lost offspring coming back into the picture. With each person I related to, I began to accept my situation as difficult but manageable. I knew that I would become a stronger person for working through my issues, as well as a stronger school psychologist.

In June of 1998, I completed my first year as a school psychologist. I also celebrated my first year with Warren, a huge success for me. As I hoped, we moved in together. Since I had the summer off—one of the many perks of working for a school district—I spent a lot of time transforming his house into our home. Warren continued to smoke outside, but I knew I couldn't put ultimatums on him. It seemed unfair to tell him I wouldn't move in until he quit, and if I could accept this little fault in him, it would help me get better in my life. I loved him and wanted to stay with him whether he smoked or not.

I took a huge step when I moved in with him. Before Warren, either I couldn't make the commitment that living together demanded because it scared me, or I did exactly the opposite and wanted to move in with a man after only three weeks of dating. In the latter cases, I would demand we get our own place because I felt that the man could kick me out at any time if I moved into his place. Of course, no one ever actually kicked me out of their home, but I never let go of the possibility because of my constant feelings of impending doom.

Needless to say, living with Warren was a big deal to me. This time, I did things different from the start. While off from work all summer, I became the happy little homemaker. We planned a trip back east to visit his family, and while he was at work, I found myself uncharacteristically cooking, sewing curtains, packing, and shopping for things we would need on our trip. I loved every minute of it.

Not long after I moved in, Warren's smoking really started to bother me. Although I noticed he had a smoker's cough before I moved in with him, it was all I could do to not cringe every time he choked on his breath. His incessant trips outside to smoke became more and more noticeable and unbearable. Though I understood addiction, I couldn't understand cigarette smoking, since I had never done it. We began to argue about it more and more and I would beg and plead with him to stop. I told him the horror stories of my adoptive mother's emphysema and how my aunt Mona had died of lung cancer on my seventeenth birthday. But I should have known better. No one could tell me what to do. What made me think I could tell someone else?

I finally realized my irritation over Warren's smoking had less to do with Warren and more to do with me. In actuality, I felt abandoned every time he went out to have a cigarette. I also feared that he would kill himself with cigarettes, and I would end up alone again. Deep down inside, I felt I had risked everything for our relationship, and all he was going to do was die on me. In hindsight, I realize how unrealistic my line of thinking was. Still, it hurt. His smoking became the only thing we really disagreed on; yet, rather than focusing on all the other good things, I could think of nothing else.

I knew he wanted to quit, and I prayed every day that God would give him the strength to do so. I tried to stay consciously grateful for the things that went well, rather than dwelling on the one thing about Warren that upset me. In general, I had a great life. I had a great job—better than my wildest dreams—and I had a precious life with Warren. Nothing better had ever happened to me. And though I missed Jeffrey, I no longer thought about him every day.

In August of 1998, I decided I wanted to locate family members on Jeffrey's side. I remembered that he'd always made it clear that most of his family didn't know I existed, and I got the distinct impression that he wanted to keep things that way. Regardless, I decided to contact my four aunts on his side of the family, and I made the decision to find Michelle, my older half sister. One day it just hit me that this was my life, and I would only get one crack at it.

I decided to contact my aunt Rebecca. I hoped she still lived in Omaha, Nebraska. I'd spoken to her once while in contact with Jeffrey, and knew he had told her all about me at the time. Of his entire family, she alone knew about me. She seemed like a good place to start.

School wouldn't start for another few weeks, and I decided this would be my summer, the one in which I would break through my family secrets and introduce myself to all my relatives. I remembered my aunt's full name, Rebecca Sobel—she, like me, had gone back to her maiden name after a divorce. Since I had misplaced her number, I called directory assistance. Luckily, she was listed and I found her easily. I called her right away and recognized her voice when she answered the phone.

"Hi," I said as my voice shook just a bit. "My name's Kasey Hamner. I'm your brother Jeffrey's daughter, your niece. You called me once, about two years ago."

I hoped she hadn't forgotten me, my lifelong fear as an adoptee. She surprised me when she answered right away.

"Hi, Kasey!" she said. "Of course I know who you are! It's good to hear from you! I've been thinking about you and have often thought about calling myself."

It thrilled me to find her so happy to hear from me. I'd dialed the phone full of dread, expecting her to hang up on me and forget about me all over again. Instead, she'd done exactly the opposite. We small-talked for a while and she told me she'd heard from Jeffrey recently. He told her that he hoped she would keep in contact with me since he didn't feel he could do so himself. As I heard these words, I wondered why she hadn't taken it upon herself to call me. Why did she wait for me to call? I was reminded of the sadness I felt when he decided to walk out of my life nearly two years ago, but also pleased that he still thought of me.

Eventually I got to the point and told Rebecca I wanted to contact my other family members and asked if she would help me. Again she surprised me and gave me the names and phone numbers of all my other aunts and her son, my cousin Dave Munson, who I learned lived less than ten miles from me. Rebecca and I promised to keep in touch, but when I hung up the phone, it struck me that no one else knew about me but Rebecca and Jeffrey. I couldn't understand why they hadn't talked to the others about me, but I knew the answer. I still remained the family secret.

I called my cousin Dave and left a vague message. I

told him that his mother, Rebecca, had suggested I call him regarding some "family business." He must have thought I was a crank caller or a saleswoman because I never got a call back. I gathered the courage to call my aunt Meredith, the one Liz had called two years earlier to inquire about Jeffrey's whereabouts. This time, I called her directly to tell her about myself. My stomach filled with butterflies as I pushed the buttons on the telephone. One ring, then two before I got her machine. After the experience I'd had when I left the message for Dave, I decided I'd rather reach her in person and hung up.

Two minutes later, my phone rang. The woman on the other end of the line told me I'd just called her home. It was Meredith. The call surprised me—I'd forgotten all about *69. I apologized for the disruption, took a deep breath, and told her I was Kasey Hamner, her long-lost niece whom her brother had given up for adoption almost thirty-one years ago. I explained quickly how he had told her family that I'd died during childbirth. I could sense her shock, even over the phone. After a brief silence, she answered only in short sentences.

I inquired about my half sister Michelle, her niece, and asked for any information she might have on how I could reach her. She told me that she had lost contact with Michelle a few years earlier, but last she heard, Michelle was married and had two children. She mentioned that Michelle's last name was Mempe, if memory served her correctly. She asked for my number and told me she'd see what she could do. I checked off the second name on my list, which became shorter as each day passed. I hoped every day that Meredith would call me back, but when a few weeks had gone by, I feared she wouldn't. I assumed she'd become busy, or possibly unsure of my true identity. I put her on the back burner and moved on. By this time, I didn't expect much. It pleased me when things progressed, but I tried to let go of all expectations. After having to let go of Jeffrey, an aunt who wouldn't return my phone call paled in comparison.

In October of 1998, I threw myself a thirty-first birthday party. It seemed somewhat strange that I used to hate celebrating birthdays, and now I threw myself a party to mark the occasion. That, I knew, was progress. The only disappointment was that Vanessa did not come to my party and she did not call me to wish me a happy birthday. All my birth relatives on Vanessa's side, with the exception of Adam, sent me multiple birthday cards and called to sing "Happy Birthday" to me over the phone. And while that was precious, I still felt horribly let down that Vanessa couldn't participate in my celebration. The more I thought about it, I realized that even though she came to the mini family reunion for my twenty-eighth birthday in Monterey and participated in the arrangement of the "rooster" telegram for my thirtieth birthday, she had never called me or wished me a happy birthday face-to-face. Thinking back, I remembered her sitting on the sidelines of the celebration while the other family members and myself happily interacted. It was almost as if it was easier for her to send me a telegram with big banners, but the intimate exchange of well-wishing was too painful for her. I know that she will never forget my birthday, but I guess it was too painful for her to acknowledge it.

As I thought about her, I surrounded myself with friends at the party, had a great time, and discovered that I really knew how to throw a party. The day after my birthday, a monumental miracle happened: Warren quit smoking! This was a huge ordeal for him. And what a gift for both of us. After trying to quit for years, and me being hard on him, he did it all on his own. It was truly a miracle.

After my birthday, I wanted to concentrate more on my relationship with Vanessa. I'd known her for four years and had never told her I loved her, though the thought had plagued me my entire life: how I could love a woman I felt had abandoned me. I wanted to tell her the moment I met her face-to-face, to embrace her and tell her I'd never given up on her, that I'd loved her and wanted to be loved by her every day of my life. But I had never actually managed to do it. In November of 1998, I decided the time had finally come. It still worried me that I might overwhelm her, but decided I needed to do it for me. Warren told me not to worry about what she might think of me, that if I loved her, I needed to tell her. "To love another is a gift to yourself," he told me again and again, and I knew he was right.

Vanessa and I went out to dinner on November 3, 1998 to celebrate both of our birthdays, mine in October and hers in December. Her brother, Mark, joined us as well. In preparation, I took Warren shopping with me to help find a gift for her, something I'd always had an awful time doing. He helped me pick out a beautiful gold clock embedded in the letters "LOVE." I thought it would send a good signal about my feelings for her, but even as I purchased the gift, Warren sensed my hesitation. Before I left to meet Vanessa and Mark for dinner, Warren reminded me to tell her exactly how I felt, and to let go of the expectations of what I hoped she would say or do.

The three of us had a wonderful meal, and when I gave her the clock, she seemed to like it. We chatted quite a bit and planned to go to a movie, but when we discovered that nothing near us started at a convenient time, we decided to go our separate ways. They walked me to my car and we talked for another ten minutes. By this time, I'd become quite nervous. I felt like a schoolgirl about to tell a boy she likes him, all giddy and anxious inside. I could have just let her leave and not said another word, but I'd made a commitment to myself to tell her I loved her that night, and one thing I'd learned over the years was the meaning of the word "love." Thoughts continued to run through my head, like, "How do you tell the woman who gave birth to you thirty-one years ago, but whom you have only known for four years, that you love her?"

When I went to hug her good-bye, I finally said it: "I love you, Vanessa." I was ready to smile, turn around, get in the car, and get over the fact that she didn't return the sentiment. Fortunately, I needn't have worried.

"I love you, too," she said.

I did it! I'd told my birth mother I loved her for the very first time, and she expressed that she loved me back! What played out between us happens maybe a billion times a day on the planet, so many times that most people forget the words before they reach the end of the sentence. But neither of us had ever experienced this. It finally hit me that she must have been afraid to tell me how she felt, but when I told her I loved her first, I gave her the opportunity to respond in kind. Maybe she felt that she didn't have a right to love me after what she'd done over three decades ago. Perhaps she'd convinced herself that I couldn't or wouldn't love her because I was so mad at her for giving me away. It's as if we had both punished ourselves by not allowing either of us to express how we really felt about each other. All my life I'd felt unlovable, and thus incapable of loving anyone, let alone my birth mother. I felt I didn't deserve to love her because she hadn't raised me. The truth is, I was angry at her, but it never had anything to do with the way I loved her.

I went home and told Warren what I'd done. He was so proud of me and I felt like I had won an Oscar. The next day, I shared with my closest friends what I'd done, and I cried my eyes out as I told them. They probably didn't understand, any of them, but I knew I had taken a risk and succeeded. How could they understand unless they had experienced it for themselves? I'd mustered up enough courage, a huge accomplishment for me. I decided my life would continue this way. I would take risks when it came to my birth family, like introducing myself to people who would otherwise never have known I existed.

The following morning, I awoke and realized that three months had passed since I called Meredith. I was convinced that she simply had no interest in knowing me. When she called me a few days later, it shocked me. She'd talked so abruptly with me the first time that I thought even if she did call back, I wouldn't get more than a name or address from her. Instead, she apologized for the delay in calling and assured me that even though her brother chose not to have contact with me, it didn't mean that she and her sisters couldn't.

As it turned out, the reason she'd reacted so distantly during our first phone conversation was because her mother, Amanda Sobel, who didn't know I existed, was sitting right next to her while we spoke. It was an enormous coincidence I called that particular day because her mother, who lived in Nebraska, hadn't visited Meredith in ten years! After we hung up, Meredith told my grandmother Amanda about me immediately. Not surprisingly, Amanda had some trouble swallowing the news. When Meredith related to me how she'd told Amanda all about me, she immediately put to rest the doubts I'd had about her not believing that I was who I said I was. Meredith told me it excited her to discover she had another niece, and she told everyone about me. That meant she had virtually completed my work with that branch of the family. Everyone knew I was alive and well and living in California. She told me that she and her twin sister, my aunt Anne, who also lived close to me, wanted to get together for dinner so we could all meet. I was ecstatic.

Nearly two weeks passed before I heard from Meredith again. She finally called on the 23rd of November, three days before Thanksgiving. We made plans to meet for dinner with Anne at my favorite Italian restaurant in the San Fernando Valley the following evening. The next day I had trouble concentrating on much of anything. I stayed at work late so I could get into the Valley without traffic, and arrived fifteen minutes early. I felt nervous about meeting new members of my birth family, yet I had an overwhelming feeling of peace and joy.

Before pulling into the parking lot, I stopped for a red light and found myself in view of the restaurant. I looked over and strained to see through the glass to someone, anyone, who looked like me, sounded like me, loved me. For the first time in my life, I would meet people from my father's side of the family. I pulled into the parking lot and looked up into an open view of the dining room. I saw a woman with dark hair who was watching the parking lot intently, and I knew immediately she was one of my aunts. When I walked in, it was as if no one else existed in the entire restaurant. I made eye contact with the dark-haired woman, who was sitting alone at a table with three menus in front of her. "Kasey?" she asked, and after I nodded in the affirmative, she said, "I'm your aunt Anne."

She smiled, stood up, and shook my hand. She had arrived early, just like me. We sat down and waited for Meredith. We talked about the adoption and I immediately felt comfortable with her. We talked like old friends who hadn't seen each other in years and had to fill each other in on our lives. She had tears in her eyes as I talked about my relinquishment and she told me about society in the 1960s and how young girls were afraid to tell anybody if they got pregnant and didn't think they could raise a child on their own. She told me she'd never had any children, and that it saddened her to know a family member hadn't raised me, even if it couldn't have been my birth mother.

Meredith arrived about twenty minutes later. Though she and Anne are twins, they look nothing alike, but in a way, I noticed they both looked a bit like me. Meredith brought lots of pictures with her, mostly of her daughter and grandchildren, my cousins. They all looked so beautiful, and I saw myself in each and every one of them. She also showed me pictures of Jeffrey's children, Simon, Autumn, and Dennis. I'd never seen pictures of any of them though Jeffrey described them to me. After all, he chose not to send me any pictures. But here, with both my aunts, there were plenty to be passed around. And with each one, my family tree grew bigger and bigger. I could feel it as it grew. In the end, it would shade me from the heat and protect me from the cold. With this awareness, the healing continued.

The three of us talked about adoption some more and they both commented on how much I look like Vanessa, and how I had her hands and Jeffrey's eyes. I'd had those hands and eyes all my life, and I'd never known who they belonged to. After we talked for hours, they walked me to my car. I felt ecstatic when they both easily told me they loved me, especially after what I'd just gone through with Vanessa. It touched and scared me at the same time. I didn't want to let them in, in case I would later have to let them go, as I'd had to do with Jeffrey.

Meredith invited me to a birthday party for her daughter Rebecca, named after my aunt Rebecca, who was turning thirty on the 30th of November. The dinner was to be held on the following Sunday. I accepted immediately and proceeded to feel nervous for the duration of the week. I planned to arrive fashionably late, so I could slip quietly into the crowd rather than wait nervously alone. As I drove to their house in

Woodland Hills, minutes away from Vanessa's home, a comforting sense of peace once again overwhelmed me. In moments, I would meet more blood relatives. I pulled just past their beautiful home and parked my car away from the house. I didn't want to park directly in front where windows lay open across the front of the house. I felt too self-conscious to have everyone watch me as I got out of the car.

I walked to the front door and rang the bell. A man opened the door and I knew right away he must be Rony, Meredith's husband.

"You must be Kasey," he said as I shook his hand. We exchanged pleasantries and I quickly felt comfortable with him just as I'd felt with Anne and Meredith. He was friendly and talkative and he introduced me to Rebecca, whose thirtieth birthday we were celebrating that day. At that very moment, I realized she'd been born on November 30, 1968, the very same day that my adoption had become finalized. It was an eerie feeling to realize that the day my adoption became complete, a cousin had been born and kept, just thirty miles away.

Rebecca introduced me to her sons: Alex, four years old, and Theo, eighteen months. I'm not sure I can possibly explain the feelings I had when I saw these two young boys, my blood relatives. I felt on the verge of tears knowing how precious they were, how beautiful. They stared at me and I stared back. They were playful with me as with every other adult in their life. If only they knew how much their presence in my life for that moment touched me to the core. Alex had beautiful green eyes, like mine. They both had the same brown hair I had, and we all shared a similar complexion. They handed me objects they had discovered around the house and repeatedly ran over to show me something that fascinated them. At one point during dinner, Alex said to me, "Kae-wee, look at my big muscles!" I could have cried tears of joy, but laughed instead and went overboard as I showed him how impressed I was with his rippling muscles.

Rebecca herself was beautiful, with gorgeous, long, thick brown hair. Her husband, Scott, was sweet and friendly. He told me his mother was adopted and didn't find her birth family until she was thirty-five. Her parents had died by then but she had maintained a beautiful relationship with her full sister since their reunion. I felt a connection to Scott when I sensed his appreciation for his mother finding her roots. He shared some of the pain that his mother went through and I was able to talk about my own pain and how I was dealing with it. I knew I would never get tired of meeting and talking to people who were touched by adoption.

I went home that night and felt somewhat sated, as if the enjoyment I'd experienced could almost make up for the pain and suffering I'd gone through over the span of my childhood. With each new relationship made in reunion, I learned more and more about myself. At thirty-one, I felt I was in the midst of passing through some rite of passage in which my own identity would reveal itself to me one layer at a time. I began to accept that I couldn't have Jeffrey in my life, and to see the potential that now lay before me with other family members who were welcoming me into their lives.

As part of my healing, my quest to develop a closer relationship with Vanessa grew stronger. Our initial "honeymoon" period had worn off two years ago, and now we didn't see each other very often. Outside of the birthday dinner we'd enjoyed in November, when I told her I loved her, the last time I'd seen her had been at her fiftieth birthday party in December of the previous year.

By this time, I'd come to an acceptance of the fact that Jeffrey was out of my life for good—and probably for the better. I realized, at length, that I needed to stop whining and complaining about what I had lost and spend more time cherishing what I still had, especially my relationship with Vanessa. It had taken me a lifetime to find her, and the last thing I wanted to do was take our relationship for granted.

About the time I resolved to improve my connection with Vanessa, I decided to write this book. I thought it would be a perfect opportunity to get to know her better, and tell her all the things I had previously withheld about my life. I wanted her, finally, to know the real me—no holds barred.

As an adult with four years of reunion under my belt, I finally accepted that Vanessa and I could never have a true mother-daughter bond because she hadn't raised me or participated in the first twenty-seven years of my life. I believe a part of me hoped she would see and treat me as her daughter.

I had to accept that I was still a secret to Vanessa's friends. I knew she hadn't told many of her friends or co-workers about me, and it bothered me that she wasn't ready to tell everyone the way I was ready to tell the world about my good fortune of having her in my life. She didn't even tell her friend of twenty years, a fellow adoptee. Vanessa told me that her friend insists she has no desire to find her birth parents because she still "hates" them, and to this day Vanessa has never told her that she gave me up for adoption. I hope one day Vanessa will want to tell the world about me. Then I won't be a secret any longer.

I wanted to be in closer contact with her, but had come to the realization that she is still a very private person. She doesn't often reach out, and rarely makes phone calls to see how I'm doing. It wasn't too long before I discovered she doesn't reach out to anybody, though I still tended to take her apparent lack of interest personally. After all, I was her long-lost daughter. I felt we had a lot of catching up to do.

She's sometimes up for going to the movies, which allows us to spend time together, but she doesn't want to talk about her emotions. I used to complain to anyone who would listen how she never called me, which of course I took to mean that she didn't want to have anything to do with me. Once I stopped complaining, I decided to keep calling her regardless. I began calling her more often, even though she never initiated calls on her own, because I knew that she would at least return calls once I made the first move. I wanted her to know me, and I would go to any lengths to make this happen. I was grateful when I realized that my plan to write this book would afford me the opportunity to spend more time with Vanessa.

Throughout my life, I dealt with feelings of rejection from Vanessa, long before I even had the chance to meet her, regardless of how real those feelings may have been. A single action was taken—she and Jeffrey gave me away—and all of us have had to deal with the aftermath for more than thirty years, the guilt and the abandonment, all of it. Ever since we'd known each other, I'd never brought any of it up because I was afraid, and I knew that she was too. For that reason, I felt connected to her.

When I began to write this book, I realized what an invaluable wealth of information she was to me. I called her when I'd made the decision to start this project. I was excited, and told her all about how I wanted to write a book about my journey of growing up adopted. I wasn't sure how she would react. I was concerned that she would not want her story told for everyone to read, especially considering how much of a secret I continued to be to everyone else in her life. Although she was hesitant about it, she supported me, knowing that it was something I needed to do.

I asked if I could come over and ask her some questions about her and my birth father, about how they met and the circumstances surrounding my relinquishment. I'd heard all this information before, several times in fact, but I wanted to be reminded. Everyone has their own story, and I was determined to hear hers again, in greater detail. I wanted her to share a part of her life with me again so that I could tell her the things I wanted her to know before she read the book. I thought back to the moment I had met her, how excited I'd been, wanting to tell her everything about my childhood, but too afraid to actually do it. Well, now was the time. I needed to take yet another risk, the risk of her rejection if she couldn't handle hearing about the things I was about to tell her.

Despite her reservations, she eventually became eager to help me. God only knows what she may have felt inside, wondering what questions I would ask, trying to anticipate the worst, afraid of losing me if she didn't respond in a certain way. I was invited to come to her house on a Saturday night for dinner, and after we ate and chatted about nothing in particular, the plates were put in the sink and out came my notebook.

Up to this juncture in our relationship, our conversations had been very superficial, aside from the first day we'd met when she explained to me the circumstances surrounding my relinquishment. But that night, she surprised me by showing a side I'd never seen before. I'd never heard her raise her voice or seen her very emotional, but when she began talking, I experienced both these things.

"All right," she said. "I'm glad to help you write this book, but there are a few things I need to tell you before we really get involved here."

I was elated to see such a response. I was all ears. She continued, "When Liz and my mother found you four years ago, it was very painful to dredge up that part of my life. There was a lot of stress for me. Good stress, but stress nonetheless." She paused for a moment. "When you located Jeffrey, I had nightmares about it for months and it was very painful for me."

I saw the truth in her eyes as she said this. I knew she was beginning to break free, to let me in a little, if only for the moment.

She sighed, took a deep breath, and said, "I'll explain to you what really happened, if that's what you want, if this is what will help you write this book. If you want me to, I'll dredge it all up again, but this is the last time."

I nodded and said okay. For the moment, I forgot all about the book and listened only to the voice before me, the voice of my birth mother, as she shared with me things saved for a moment alone with her daughter. She said she'd tell me everything as long as I changed her name in the book, which I'd already decided to do anyway. I let her know there were things that I needed to say to her as well, but we decided she'd start. Finally, after so many years, the truth unraveled before me.

I began to ask questions. She answered as if on a witness stand, succinctly but completely. She told me again about how she'd met my father, and the difficulties they'd had dealing with a pregnancy before their marriage. She told me how her parents, my grandparents, did not approve of Jeffrey and how they felt he was a bad influence on her.

Her voice suddenly dropped to a whisper. "Kasey," she said. "There are some things that I have not told you about Jeffrey. I was afraid to tell you anything negative about him because I know how much he means to you. But the truth is that our marriage was not all honey and roses." She hesitated. "Do you want to hear the whole truth?"

I immediately said, "Yes."

She began, "Two years after we gave you up for adoption, Jeffrey felt the need to find himself and made plans to move to France. He'd heard they were desperate for teachers at a certain school there and thought he would go there to get his credential. I knew he'd never follow through with his plan, but I went along with it anyway. He would go over first, then supposedly send for me when he was settled. Well, he never did. Instead, he traveled all over Europe, occasionally wiring me for more money. I basically financed his excursion to find himself. My friends told me I was an idiot for sending him money, but I continued to do so. A year later, after being unable to find himself to his satisfaction, Jeffrey returned from Europe and began to drink and use drugs heavily. He was always out of a job and became violent when he was under the influence of drugs and alcohol. This went on for about four years.

"One evening, close to the time of our seventh anniversary, Jeffrey was in a fit of rage after coming home drunk. He pushed me up against a wall, accused me of having an affair, called me a slut and every other name in the book, and forced me to have sex with him without my diaphragm. The following morning, I realized I had finally had enough and I began proceedings to become legally separated."

I couldn't believe it. I guess I always wondered what had broken up my birth parents' marriage, but I never imagined this.

"A week later I started having an intimate relationship with Wyatt, a man from work whom I'd felt attracted to for years. I never acted on it earlier because I took my marriage vows seriously. When I discovered I was pregnant with your brother Adam two weeks later, I assumed that Jeffrey was the father since I'd always used birth control with Wyatt. Adam was born while our divorce was still pending, and Jeffrey, not knowing that I had been with another man, also assumed Adam was his son. So Jeffrey's name appeared on Adam's birth certificate as the father. Somehow—I will never know how—Jeffrey found out that I had been with Wyatt a week after the initial separation, and demanded that we take a blood test to prove his paternity. Amazingly enough, the test results showed that Adam was Wyatt's son! So much for the reliability of birth control!

"As Adam approached his toddler years, he became a carbon copy of Wyatt, so much so that Jeffrey, feeling betrayed, decided he couldn't handle being in the same state as me and moved away, never to be heard from again until you found him two years ago. Wyatt hung around for a few years, never revealing his true identity to Adam, and died suddenly of a heart attack when Adam was five. Because Jeffrey's name appeared on Adam's birth certificate and I was still legally married to Jeffrey when Adam was born, I decided not to tell him the truth. I didn't want to disrupt his life and have him believe he was a bastard. I didn't tell Adam the true identity of his real father until he was twenty years old —the same time I told him he had a sister—you!"

So until the age of twenty, my half brother Adam thought that he had been abandoned by his birth father, Jeffrey, when in reality his true father, Wyatt, had remained with him until he died. Hearing this story made me melancholy. I realized that Adam and I had even more in common than I originally thought—the theme of betrayal of trust ran through our lives. It now made perfect sense why Adam didn't want to hear anything about his father Wyatt, my birth father Jeffrey, or the circumstances surrounding my adoption—it was probably too painful for him. It now made perfect sense that whenever I—always eager to bond with my half brother—mentioned the father we supposedly shared in common, he would abruptly change the subject, claiming he didn't care that he never had a chance to know his father. It made me sad to realize how bitter and hurt Adam must have been, knowing that it all could have been avoided if only Vanessa had been honest with him from the beginning. I couldn't blame him.

Now I learned that my birth mother was abused by my birth father—one of the nightmares I used to have growing up. Maybe I sensed it as a child and that is why I starting having the nightmares as a young child? Who knows. It is not all that uncommon for birth families to be connected in such a way despite years of separation.

Now that Vanessa had shared her horror stories with me, I felt it was time to tell her my story. But before I revealed the truth to Vanessa about my adoptive family, I reminded her how important it was that she was in my life. I knew we couldn't be mother and daughter in the traditional sense, but at the very least, we could be friends. I told her I wanted her to know the truth about me, the whole truth. I felt she had a right to know. Deep inside, I acknowledged that the abuse from Todd never would have happened had I not been put up for adoption. But I realized now that my life would not have been perfect even if my birth parents had raised me. I finally understood that no family is perfect.

I explained there were things about my childhood I'd never told her, and she said she was ready to listen. I knew I had to be honest with her. It was the first step toward a candid, truthful relationship with my birth mother.

I took a deep breath, and started at the beginning. I told her about the molestation, and how I turned to food for solace. I told her how my adoptive mother restricted my food intake. I told her about the attempted drowning incident. I told her about the "misdemeanor list." I told her how my adoptive mother refused to acknowledge that her firstborn son molested me over a span of ten years. I told her about the drinking, the drugs, and the stealing. I told her how sad I was when Todd molested me, and how I'd cried myself to sleep, night after night, praying to God she'd come and get me. "I was mad at you!" I told her. "But most of all, I loved you."

Although she was shocked, she was very supportive and thankful that I finally told her the truth. She asked me questions, and I answered them truthfully. She asked if I was going to put it all in the book, and I said yes. "Tell the truth," she said, and we made a pact—no more secrets between us.

I felt like the weight of the world had been lifted from my shoulders. The relief was indescribable. Finally, she knew. She knew the truth about me. The good, the bad, the spectacular, and the horrible.

After our visit, Vanessa called to tell me something else about my relinquishment that might be useful for my book. Each time she called, I became more and more grateful for our talk. It was apparently the right thing to do. The truth really does set you free. A few weeks after our heart-to-heart talk, Vanessa asked me if I thought Adam had a problem with alcohol and drugs as she had developed some concerns lately. I explained to her that only Adam could determine if he had a drinking problem. Without revealing the specifics of that Fourth of July evening more than three years before, I told her his behavior mirrored my own behavior until I got sober. She asked me if I could talk to him and I assured her that I would be more than happy to, but that it was his responsibility to come to me.

Four and a half years after my birth family found me, I decided that I wanted to find my half sister Michelle, Jeffrey's daughter. Up to this point, many walls had arisen in my path, but I refused to surrender until I found her. I'd tried the Internet, 1-800-US-SEARCH, and asked family members to help. 1-800-US-SEARCH only wasted my time and money. They told me they needed a birth date in order to find her. Various family members, especially Meredith, said they would help me, but did not follow through.

Liz, as always, tried to help but also encountered many obstacles. I thought about contacting Jeffrey again, just to find out Michelle's birth date, not to have any kind of relationship with him. Just the thought of that dredged up those old feelings again, and I felt uncomfortable. But I decided to give it a shot. I attempted to call his home and work numbers that I had, but it turned out that he had moved and changed jobs, which he apparently did quite often, so my luck ran out in that arena. My luck turned when I attended one of my support group meetings for adoptees.

At that meeting I heard another adoptee say he had found out information about his birth mother through the help of an independent search consultant—a birth mother who helps members of the adoption triad reunite. I asked for the number and called her the following day. The consultant was a very nice lady who worked as a volunteer and asked only for reimbursement of her expenses. I gave her all the information I had about Michelle. I knew she'd been born Michelle Sobel, adopted as Michelle Doner, and had supposedly married and taken the last name of Mempe. I told her that Michelle was born probably in 1962 or 1963, since I was told she was four at the time of my birth in October of 1967. She asked me if her birth had occurred in Los Angeles County. I thought for a moment and remembered that Jeffrey, who fathered Michelle in high school, had gone to school in the San Fernando Valley, which is part of Los Angeles County.

Therefore, we could safely assume that the answer to that question was yes.

The searcher told me that she would begin the search immediately, but it might take a week or two to find Michelle. I thanked her profusely and felt a great sense of accomplishment that I had finally found somebody who could help me. I eagerly went about my day, confident that I would soon have the exact location and contact information for my sister Michelle. I could hardly think straight. Could my wish come true?

The searcher called me back less than a half hour later. She asked me if I had a pen and paper, then proceeded to tell me that she had located a Michelle Sobel Doner Mills (not Mempe as I was told by Meredith) in San Dimas, California, only forty-five minutes from me! She gave me her birth date, which was January 16, 1963, her mailing address, work and home phone numbers, and the name of her husband, Lenny Mills. I couldn't believe it. My parents adopted me on her fifth birthday! In a half hour, she found what the Internet and 1-800-US-SEARCH couldn't touch. I couldn't thank her enough.

My head spun with how quickly it had all happened. Then I realized that now that I had Michelle's information, I didn't know how I should handle it. I asked the searcher what she thought I should do. Should I write her a letter or call her? Fear of rejection crept up on me again, and I found myself worrying about upsetting the applecart. I knew that Michelle had no idea I even existed, just like the rest of my father's side of the family. The searcher told me it was up to me, although she recommended that if I did decide to make contact, I should call. It would mean more, she thought, if Michelle could hear my voice instead of just reading a letter. I thanked her again and asked if she might find the birth dates of my other three half siblings on my birth father's side, Simon, Autumn, and Dennis. I wanted to have their birth dates so that when they turned eighteen, I could locate them as well. She was willing to locate the dates and get back to me when she succeeded.

I attempted to return to my work, but this time I couldn't get anything done. I went home and eagerly waited for Warren to return. When he arrived, he asked how my day had gone. I casually replied, "I had a good day, no big deal," then paused for effect. "Oh, by the way," I added nonchalantly, "I found Michelle today." His face lit up like a Christmas tree. My news both shocked and pleased him, and he said he looked forward to seeing what would happen. I didn't sleep at all that night. I knew that the next day I would have to either write the letter or make the call. If I didn't, I would never be able to concentrate on my duties. Still, I didn't know what to do. My mind raced as the committee inside my head tried to reach a decision.

After much debate, I opted to write a letter. I convinced myself that a letter would be less intrusive than a phone call. I explained who I was and that I had reason to believe we were sisters. I loaded the letter with facts so that she wouldn't have any doubts about my true identity. I gave her my address and phone numbers at work and at home. I wrote draft after draft until I became satisfied with the results, then excitedly mailed the letter off to San Dimas. That was March 16, 1999.

I eagerly waited for a reply, but none came. Three weeks passed and I decided to call, in case she hadn't received the letter. I called and left a message on the business line at her home, but did not get a response. Almost two months passed and she still hadn't called. I refused to believe she would choose not to contact me, and became convinced that I had erroneous information. In the meantime, I contacted 1-800-US-SEARCH and gave them Michelle's birth date just to make sure that I had the right person, and also so they could earn the fee I had already paid them. When I got the results, I felt confounded. They did in fact locate Michelle, but found three different addresses in San Dimas under her name. My curiosity and doubt flourished once again.

After a few days, it began to drive me crazy that I didn't know whether or not she got the letter. I decided to ask someone to act as an intermediary to contact her and find out. I called Warren and told him what I wanted to do. He agreed one hundred percent that I had to know one way or the other, and suggested that I ask a friend from my adoptee support group to call her. I hung up the phone with Warren and called my friend Tina; she was always articulate when it came to getting through uncomfortable situations. When I reached her machine, I remembered that she had left town for a week. I knew that I couldn't wait that long, and since I could not think of anybody else that I trusted more than Warren, I called him back and asked him to make the call for me.

Warren paged Michelle from his office and waited for a return call. Two minutes later he received a call from Lenny Mills, Michelle's husband. As it turned out, the pager belonged to their family business and Lenny had it on that day. Warren introduced himself and told Lenny that he had called on my behalf. He had barely finished his sentence when Lenny exclaimed, "Thank God you called, Warren. I've wanted to call for weeks now!" He proceeded to tell Warren that Michelle had in fact received the letter and the phone message. He explained that my attempts to make contact had shocked her, and she simply couldn't yet deal with the situation. Lenny sounded very concerned about Michelle but said it pleased him to learn that she had a sister. When Michelle received the letter, he suggested she call right away so we could meet, but she was simply unable to. Lenny told Warren to assure me that her decision not to respond had nothing to do with me. Warren and Lenny talked for a few minutes and ended the conversation once they decided that I should not contact her anymore. The ball was truly in her court; it was up to her to contact me.

When Warren recounted the conversation, I burst into tears and asked him, "What do I do now?" He gave me the only advice he could: "Let it go." What else could I do? It felt like nothing else would allow me to move on with my life. I tried to think of all the reasons that she might not want to have contact with me. I remembered that we had both been given up for adoption by the same man, had both reunited as adults, she in person, me by phone, and we had both lost contact with him. I thought perhaps she couldn't endure the eventual pain that often results from reunion. Worse yet, maybe she simply didn't have any interest in knowing me.

Meanwhile, I had to deal with my own feelings. Yes, I felt rejected. Yes, I took it personally that she wouldn't contact me. Most of all, I felt terribly sad that once again the secrecy of adoption had reared its ugly head. I experienced anger and sadness simultaneously. I went home that night and cried with Warren and anybody else who would listen to me. I went to bed and slept like a log, probably because I'd finally released all the anxiety about the status of my sister Michelle and me. I woke up the next morning and felt an amazing sense of relief. I had accomplished what I had set out to accomplish when I told her that she had a sister. She had reacted with shock, but I had completed the task nonetheless. One more member of my birth family knew that I existed. That knowledge alone continued the healing process.

Chapter 8

Life on Life's Terms

After years of attending workshops, receiving quality therapy from an adoption triad member, reading extensive adoption literature, studying the field of psychology, being in a trusting relationship with Warren, and simply experiencing the passage of time, I have finally been able to develop valuable insights and perspective regarding my adoption situation and family members.

As an adult adoptee in reunion, I accept that I will always be in the reunion process. Some days seem easier than others, even still. In fact, some hours are easier than others, and sometimes I live more by the minute than by the day. I struggle to change my attitudes on the issues of my adoption, and I am still prone to having difficulties with relationships. The most important thing I've learned is that I'm an adult, and the first person I need to take care of is me. Though my issues surrounding my adoption have no cure, I can now see that the pain and fear of abandonment diminish with time. To date, no panacea exists, though some things make me feel better. I still fear abandonment and deal with bouts of depression, but I always come back stronger and more assured.

As an adoptee, my fear of rejection discouraged me from risk taking. I've conquered most of that fear now in my life and my thirst for challenge has brought forth many risks. The biggest of these was my involvement in a real, strong, trusting, and loving relationship. I often hear people talk about how they're working on themselves. "I'll eventually get into a relationship," they say, "but I'm not ready now." While I've also been guilty of this thought process, I now believe the one surefire way to work on yourself is in a relationship. I don't mean casual dating or the kind of relationship where one person likes the other more, or a relationship devoid of trust and intimacy. Rather, I mean a solid, intimate, committed, monogamous relationship with someone you love.

In all the fly-by-night relationships I had with men I didn't trust, who I felt unattracted to, or who scared me, of course I wouldn't let my true colors show. Why bother to open myself up when I knew I wouldn't stay around long enough? I knew I'd never reap the benefits of dealing with my issues. Now, I benefit from the hard work I've put into my relationship with Warren. Being in a long-term, committed relationship is one of the hardest things I've ever done, and I'm doing it successfully. I've found no better place to deal with my issues.

No one knows me as well as Warren—no one. He is my best friend and confidant. I still test and retest his love for me and commitment to me in insecure ways if I start to feel abandoned or lonely. I especially have a hard time when I hear him coughing incessantly, something that has continued even after he quit smoking. At times I fear the worst—that he will get sick and die. And death has always been exceptionally difficult for me to handle. I always take longer to recover than your average person. I know now that the only way to overcome my fears is to continue in the relationship as long as I remain happy, keep admitting my faults, keep working on myself, and admit when I behave childishly so I can continue to grow up. I also know that even if Warren and I split up, I will not be abandoned by him. Our relationship will simply change.

Searching for extended-family members who thought I had died at birth has healed me the most. Whether that search results in a relationship is irrelevant. I firmly believe that there are crucial reasons why certain people are not in my life. I recommend that all adoptees search for their family. If their biological parents are unable to put in the time required to have a relationship with them, it's more than likely that a plethora of other relatives out there are able to do so. Only God knows how my relationships will develop, but every one has begun with a phone call, a letter, or a meeting. When my three younger siblings Dennis, Simon, and Autumn reach eighteen, I plan to search for them as well.

Being able to see myself reflected in my birth family is priceless. My found relatives answered my medical questions and validated many of my idiosyncrasies. I no longer have to say "I don't know" when a doctor asks me about my family history. I now know that I have breast cancer, diabetes, high blood pressure, and depression in my family. All of this knowledge helps explain my hypoglycemia and episodes of depression. I also don't feel so alone when I know that Vanessa suffers from migraines, vertigo, and TMJ—just like me. I don't feel like a freak so much anymore. I stand out in my adoptive family in terms of physical characteristics, creativity, preferences, and temperament. But I fit right in with my birth family. My emotionality, talents, and predispositions fall right in line with them. And while I may wish I had deeper relationships with some of them, I feel in my heart that there is a connection. Learning the reasons for my relinquishment, while initially painful, has benefited me in the long run. I no longer fantasize or have nightmares about why my parents gave me up. I know they created me in love and released me due to fear and societal pressures. This doesn't excuse anything, but at least it explains things.

I know now of my impact on others, and that it can be used for good or bad. I feel that I have the capability to make people feel good about themselves, especially children. I have been told that my sense of humor brings people together. My greatest hope is that I can make a difference.

I want to impact people in good ways rather than bad. Regardless of the status of my relationships or whether I've come up against another wall in my search for family members, I have to treat the people I love with respect. I have to remind myself that Warren is separate from those I feel have abandoned me, that my pain is not his fault. I find myself lashing out at him merely because of his proximity. Whoever said "you only hurt the one you love" was right on.

It heals me to get involved with the adoption community. I attend seminars, lectures, and plays, and keep in contact with other members of the adoption triad. I continue to reach out to other adoptees. I share my triumphs and tragedies with people who truly understand me. I discuss my relationship issues, which continue to surface, and the parts of my life most adversely affected by my adoption issues. I also discuss my post-reunion issues and the life challenges of living adopted. I enjoy spending time with other adoptees and others concerned with the lifelong effects of adoption.

Recently I attended a lecture on "The Dual Reality of Adoption." I found it very healing to sit in a roomful of people as they worked on healing from the insidious issues of being adopted. At my adoptee meetings, people share parts of their stories, and I connect to them at a cellular level. To witness others heal helps me heal.

Since I decided to write this book, I discovered how supportive the adoption community is. They see the importance for all members of the triad to tell their version of the truth of adoption. They acknowledge the differences in every story, and their need to be told. Today the adoption community continues to expand, even into universities, which have begun to offer courses in adoption studies. One day, I hope to see master's and doctoral programs in adoption studies. I feel there can never be too many people involved in this area. The more ways there are to learn, the more ways there are to heal.

I've always enjoyed journal writing. If I hadn't, I never could have remembered all the details and dates of my life. Once I made a commitment to myself to write every day, I didn't stop. Writing down my feelings on paper or typing them into the computer is extremely cathartic and safe. After all, paper and keyboards don't have feelings and will never judge me for mine. When I write, I always have the courage to say things I could never say out loud. If I find myself afraid to say something to someone, I take out the paper and write it down. After many drafts, I no longer feel the need to talk to that person, or have worked through the anger to a point where I can calmly communicate with them.

This all said, writing this book has obviously been the most healing thing I could do for myself, and hopefully, other members of the triad will benefit. The ultimate healing experience is to get the truth out. After all, secrets kill. So when I let it out, when I cry and scream, I heal.

I continue to see a counselor on a regular basis. Most recently I have found a clinical psychologist who is in the adoption triad. Her knowledge and sensitivity to adoption issues have helped me profoundly. She has helped me see parts of myself that I never knew existed. She helped me see how much both my adoptive and birth families have helped mold me into who I am today. She has helped me move past the pain and into the realm of forgiveness. She has helped foster strength in me in order to repair and resolve the relationships that plagued me. She is the first psychologist I have trusted and have made a commitment to see on a regular basis.

I firmly believe in talk therapy. My belief stems from the many benefits I've received from attending therapy, not merely from the fact that I became a psychologist myself. In the past, I constantly withheld information from my therapists. Most of my therapists didn't know how to deal with me, so I didn't know how to tell them how I felt. I now recognize honesty as the catalyst for healing.

Professionally, I love working with adoptive families, adopted children, and those who have been abandoned in some way. My students don't know I'm adopted, but I believe they relate better to me because I know what they're going through, and even parents tell me I've reached a level of trust with their adopted child that no one else could. I have recently had to deal with many adoptive parents who were extremely neglectful of their adopted children. I am used to dealing with neglectful parents in general, but when I come up against an adoptive parent who states in front of their child that they don't want them anymore and want to send them back to the agency, I have to explain to the parent that their adopted child may simply be acting out his or her fears of being sent back to test if the parent will give up on them. I explain that the child is afraid of being abandoned again and is simply trying to get their attention. To the adopted child, negative attention is better than none at all. I try to help those parents realize that each time they threaten their adopted child with being sent back, they are further traumatizing that child.

On the other hand, I have also been blessed with adoptive parents who truly take great pride in raising their adopted children. When they ask me questions about their adopted child's unique issues, I explain to them that their child is traumatized, and that no matter how wonderful they are as parents, there is nothing they can do to take the pain away. I remind them that they can never take the place of the birth mother, and should never try to. I tell them to be the best parents they can be, and to be there for their adopted child as the child comes to terms with his or her pain. I emphasize the importance of being consistent with love and affection, boundaries, and following through on a promise. I want them to understand that every let down, no matter how minor, can feel like a major abandonment to the adoptee.

I tell them to expect that there are going to be days when the adoptee will test their patience and require a little extra tender loving care. For instance, on the adoptee's birthday, I suggest to parents that they allow their adopted child to express his or her feelings surrounding that especially painful day, and perhaps celebrate "adoption day" as well. I warn them that because a birthday is often a day of mourning for the adoptee, that child needs extra love and support on and around that day as assurance that the adoptive parents are glad the child is alive and part of their family. It is the ultimate dichotomy. The adoptee hates that their birthday comes around once a year, wishes that it could be forgotten, but desperately needs that day to be acknowledged. The child wants everybody to remember their birthday, and even if an insignificant person in their life forgets the day, it can feel like a dagger through their heart.

I encourage adoptive parents to nurture and support their adopted child's uniqueness and individuality. I remind them that their child has a unique genetic package and will therefore have fundamental differences that need to be acknowledged and nurtured. I encourage them to allow their adopted child to ask questions about their heritage, and to subsequently support the child's curiosity about their roots.

I emphasize that adoptive parents should always tell their child that he or she is adopted. When the child inevitably asks why, I suggest that they refrain from saying it was because the child was loved by the birth parents. I recommend that they explain the reasons for the relinquishment in as simple terms as possible—always remembering to honor the adoptee's feelings, affirming that they are valid. I emphasize that just because the adopted child cannot remember the separation from the birth mother, it doesn't make it any less devastating. For example, I tell parents to say things like, "You must be very sad that your birth parents could not raise you. I know it is confusing to you when we explain that your birth parents did what they thought was right for you. We understand that all you feel is hurt, no matter the reasons."

I consider myself a spiritual person rather than a religious one. God helps me move past the low self-esteem and shame about what Todd did to me, and the pain of how my adoptive mother treated me while my adoptive father let it happen. God now helps me change from unlovable to lovable. Through him, I became a creative, sensitive person who does estimable things. I try not to blame God for all the evils in my life and believe that He does not let things happen. God simply helps me deal with life on life's terms.

Before recovery, I lived from paycheck to paycheck and went from one unfulfilling relationship to another because I didn't think I deserved better. I never intended to know my birth family, go back to graduate school, live with the man of my dreams, have a job of my dreams, and live the kind of life I wanted. I believe one hundred percent that there is no way I could have gone through my reunion and its aftermath without God, support groups, and recovery. In October of 1994, when I decided to search in June of 1997, I believe God knew that the reunion was going to take place on December 5, 1994, and He was planting the thoughts in my mind so that I would be somewhat prepared to deal with it.

Even though there were times when I didn't think I could handle hearing the truth, in the long run I know that the truth has truly set me free. Even though there was no preparation for learning that my birth relatives thought I was dead, I am grateful that I had the foundation of recovery and therapy to bring me to the point in my life where my reunion was manageable. God truly had a much better plan for me than I ever could have imagined for myself. I am sometimes amazed at how my life has turned out, in spite of or because of my history. A truer miracle is that I now want the things I deserve.

I pray and meditate daily to pamper myself and nurture my spirituality. I am far from an expert on either subject, but they work, even in their most rudimentary stages. Every night, I spend quality time with Warren in our Jacuzzi, while our two basenjis chase each other in the yard. After this, I sit in my favorite quiet place. First I read my favorite meditation book, which includes positive affirmations for women. Then I read some sort of spiritual literature and perhaps do some journal writing, which often consists of a gratitude list for the day. I also take this time to pray that God will lift my obsessions, and to thank Him for bringing my birth family to me. Then I pray to the universe that individuals like my adoptive mother, birth father, and Vanessa receive all the peace and serenity that every human being deserves.

No one needs to know when I pray, which makes it special to me. I can do it in the car, in the shower, in my office, first thing in the morning, and during my quiet time at night. After I read and pray, I turn off the light and listen to my own breath—in, out, in, out, in, out, in, out. I attempt to focus my mind on the sounds around me, such as the rain or the sound of silence.

When thoughts and worries of the day clutter my mind, I ask my higher power to "empty my head and fill up my soul." This also helps when I have trouble sleeping because my head refuses to stop going a mile a minute. I attempt to listen to God and my own intuition. I have come to the conclusion that I am more than anything I have ever called myself, more than anything I have ever thought I was. I am more than just my name or my title, whether it's girlfriend or somebody's daughter. I am a child of God. I may have been born without a known history, but I have a purpose. God does not create junk, and I am meant to be here.

The hardest thing I've attempted is to take "contrary action." When I feel the onset of depression, I acknowledge my experiences and remind myself I am neither an infant nor a little girl and I can make my own choices. I allow myself time to grieve, then remind myself the moment will pass. When I begin to sabotage my success or happiness, I try to step back, look at the situation, and remind myself that no one will abandon me again. They may leave my life, but I will not be abandoned. Then I do or say the exact opposite of how I am feeling. I call this "self-talk." When I feel unlovable, I say to myself, "You are the most lovable person on the planet!" or "God loves you as much as He loves all of His creatures!" When I begin to feel like a freak of nature because I don't look like my adoptive family, I look at pictures of my birth family and remember I look like a lot of people. And when I feel like someone will abandon me around the next turn, I say to myself, "These feelings are not welcome here anymore." This all might sound simplistic and sophomoric, but it really does work, and I strongly suggest it to others to help break the cycles of destructive thinking.

It's all about taking my power back. I had no power over my destiny as a baby, and now I can take that power back. Of course, this is much easier said than done, but it's important to know that I can do it. When I get into a bad spot, it can feel impossible to take contrary action. It's as if I suddenly develop amnesia about how great my life is, how I have all the support I need and am never alone. Self-talk comes difficult at first, but it's very valuable, and it works.

I also try to do things that scare me, like taking emotional risks. For example, when Warren and I started to date and he took me to that hotel resort at the beach for a week, I realized that it was the same town that Todd had once lived in for years. Normally, I would never go anywhere near a place he'd been. But this time, I made a decision to create my own existence and enjoy happy vibes in a place that could have stirred negative feelings in me. I asked Warren to drive me around town so we could leave our positive energy and spirit there. It worked! We had a wonderful time and planned to return soon.

Another emotional risk for me is to let people into my life. I have succeeded with Warren by letting him into my life, and after fifteen years of wanting dogs, I decided to adopt two basenjis, who remind me of my beloved basenji Sharka who was put to sleep on my seventeenth birthday. Up to this point I did not want to risk loving and then inevitably losing an animal. One thing I have learned is that in order to feel a loss, you have to have gained something.

A great example of this is what happened two months after I adopted them. Apparently, the meter maid was coming to read our gas meter and left the gate open. My two basenjis, through no fault of their own, took off, most likely very excited about their chance for adventure. I felt as if my worst nightmare was coming true. Here I was willing to take the risk of yet another emotional attachment to something that I could lose, and they were gone. I thought I had lost two souls that had become a very important part of my life. As I prepared the "lost dogs" signs and drove around the neighborhood looking for them, all I could do was pray that they would return safely. Five hours later they miraculously returned on their own. They actually found their way home after only two months with me. What this ordeal taught me was how much I truly love my dogs and how grateful I am that I brought them into my life in the first place. It also reminded me how deeply I experience losses, no matter how minor. I am simply more sensitive than your average person, and that is all right.

All the things I've mentioned here help me day by day, minute by minute. I have no other goal than to become the best person I can, in each and every area of my life. I took the biggest step when I recognized I needed help to succeed. Years of taking my own advice proved disastrous, so as I encountered helpful people along the way, I enlisted their help in my battle against me. This way, I can live happily, not just as an adoptee but as a loving, feeling human being. I only hope that I can continue to remind myself that God will love me, even when I feel unlovable.

I now accept that Vanessa did what she thought was right over thirty-two years ago. There are still times when I ask myself if the pain will ever go away. The answer I offer to myself is that I will probably always be sad on my birthday when Vanessa doesn't call me. A part of me will always want her to tell her friends about me. Deep down I know I have a hard time accepting the fact that I am her child—born in wedlock—that she didn't raise, even though she kept Adam—born out of wedlock. I don't have to like these circumstances, but it benefits me to accept it. I love her very much, and now realize that she simply may not want to connect with me. After all, it must not be easy to share her pain with the very person that is a constant reminder of it.

I do, however, accept that I no longer have to feel at fault for the relinquishment. I did nothing wrong. The longer I am in reunion with her and the more I talk to other birth parents, the more I see that her guilt is paralyzing, even though I don't blame her anymore. The fact of the matter is that our relationship is the most complex of all—we are blood-tied but we don't know each other. We have the same body type, identical hands and handwriting, and same health issues, yet we are strangers to each other. I was reminded recently that we haven't spent the amount of time together that is required to develop a strong relationship. I am willing to put in the hours and hope that someday Vanessa will be willing to do the same. I try to remind myself that while we don't see each other often, she has made herself available for many important celebrations in my life. I remain forever grateful that she came to my graduation ceremony and party, and supported me through the initial trauma of losing Jeffrey. For the most part, I try to accept her in her entirety. For now, I call when I want to hear her voice, something that has always soothed me.

Vanessa probably loves me more than I will ever know. Most importantly, throughout the relationship with the woman who gave me life, I remind myself that it's all right to want a relationship with my birth mother. It makes me happy to know her. It thrills me to look like her. And, finally, it especially pleases me that she knows the truth about my life. For now she is in my life, and only time will tell how our relationship will develop over the years.

My grandmother Elaine and I still keep in touch. She calls me periodically, just to see how I'm doing, and I always love to hear from her. She still lives in Monterey, where she moved shortly after we first met. She's a fantastic lady who I love very much. I will never forget she's the person who found me, the first birth relative I talked to. For that reason, she holds a very special place in my heart. Even though two generations separate us and she doesn't always understand the things that I do, she always makes herself available to listen to me and support me. I hope that she gets as much of a kick out of simply hearing my voice on the other end of the line as I do when I hear hers. I do not think I will ever get tired of hearing the voices of those I am related to by blood. Every so often, I thank her for taking the time to find me and for thinking about me all of my life.

L iz and I remain very close. We talk often. And when we do, we inevitably have marathon conversations. We share so much in common in nearly every aspect and people have told me I look more like her than Vanessa. I agree, though I have many similarities with Vanessa as well. Liz has become the one whom I have connected to the most over the years. I continue to connect with her the way I dream of connecting with Vanessa someday. I feel I can talk to her about anything. She is a wonderful listener, which makes her an invaluable friend. I never forget that she is the greatest search assistant and intermediary around. I love her dearly.

Since I met my brother Adam on Christmas day in 1994, not much has happened between us. We used to talk on the phone and visit during the holidays, but today we only keep in touch by e-mail, if at all. I'll never forget the times we spent together during those first holidays, and the fact that he drove twelve hours to come to my graduation ceremony and party.

I would be remiss if I didn't mention that my relationship with Adam is less than what I had hoped it would become. It saddened me when I realized that our shallow conversations always consisted of his drinking stories, which more often than not caused him to laugh hysterically. Believe me, I didn't find the stories funny in the least, especially because I could relate to them and knew from firsthand experience what that sort of life can lead to.

Adam and I never talk about reality. We never discuss the fact that I am his sister, given up by our mother, and that he didn't even know he had a sister until a few months before we met. It's as if he is still afraid to look at the truth. The fact is that our mother kept his true father and my existence a secret from him until he was twenty years old. I can only imagine what it must be like to find out that the man you thought was your father didn't really abandon you because he wasn't your father after all, even though his name is on your birth certificate. And then, to top it off, you find out your real father is dead and has been for years. I look forward to the future, and hope we can develop a meaningful relationship where we can discuss each other's lives and the pain surrounding the secrecy of adoption and betrayal. After all, he's the only other person who came from the same womb as I did and we have the same names for mother and father listed on our birth certificates—my original one, that is.

Over three years have passed since I last spoke to Jeffrey. Thankfully, with the passage of time and perspective, I realize now that my insatiable desire to be loved by my birth father rendered me blind. I now see that the nature of our brief relationship was inappropriate and I was operating on feelings and emotions that prevented me from seeing what was happening. When he told me to call him whenever I wanted, I took advantage of that. On the other hand, he was a grown man with a family—he had no business being on the phone with me five times a day. I didn't realize back then that I was holding on desperately to the idea that we would meet someday. The constant phone calls were just my way of holding on to a piece of Jeffrey—a piece I thought I deserved.

Although he never explained to me the reasons for cutting me out of his life, I believe that his wife, Pat, felt betrayed by him—rightly so, and he simply didn't want to lose his third family. I can respect that today. At the time, he was leading me on with the constant attention and I was eating it up. I was being dangled by him in that I was waiting for us to meet and he kept delaying. It wasn't my fault. I was not a bad person, only a daughter who wanted to fill a void that could not and should not be filled by just one human being—especially not my birth father. What was I thinking—that he could take away all my pain?

If I could do it all again, I would have discontinued the phone calls and arranged to have a meeting with his family present. No secrets. I realize now that typical reunions consist of the initial phone call and, in most cases, a subsequent meeting. He told me many times that we were going to meet and I held on to the hope of meeting my birth father and half siblings with every waking breath. I believe that I was simply trying to create a reunion, and didn't see that there was something wrong with the way he was relating to me. In actuality, his withdrawal from our relationship was a blessing in disguise and probably the most mature action he could've taken. It's true what they say about time healing all wounds. I never believed that would be true in my case, but it has gotten easier over the years.

After all is said and done, I am now open to having contact with Jeffrey again. I still want to meet my birth father and I don't believe that desire will ever go away. It is okay for me to want to meet my half siblings as well. In the future, when and if the reunion occurs, it would have to be under very different circumstances.

I will confront him about the nature of our previous relationship and I will let him know in no uncertain terms that his wife and family need to be present when we meet. I want Pat to be completely comfortable with the situation, otherwise I will not participate in a reunion with him.

As I create my own life and world, I try to accept the fact that just because I want a relationship with someone doesn't mean they want the same thing. However, I wish to emphasize that it is a tragedy to initiate contact or start a relationship with a child you relinquished for adoption if you don't intend to see the relationship through, in all of its ups and downs. Unless the relationship is abusive or inappropriate, there is no reason why reunited relatives can't be a part of each other's lives. If the relationship does become inappropriate, like Jeffrey's and mine was, it doesn't mean that adjustments can't be made and boundaries can't be set. I never want to experience that kind of loss again, and I hope nobody else ever has to.

The same holds true for extended-family members. As it turns out, none of my relatives on Jeffrey's side of the family have reciprocated contact with me. Since I last saw them at Rebecca's birthday party dinner in November of 1998, I have not heard from my aunt Anne, aunt Meredith, or my aunt Rebecca back in Omaha. This situation is baffling to me since all of my aunts, except for my aunt Kari, who I haven't had any contact with, professed their love for me, gratitude for knowing me, and desire to develop a relationship with me. They all claimed they wanted to have a relationship with me despite the fact that their brother, my birth father, was unable to continue to do so. After frequent attempts on my part to make contact, I have not heard from any of them. So, like everything else, I have to let them go, accepting the fact that for some unknown reason I am not meant to have them in my life right now.

In dealing with all the realities of reunion, and the fact that I have been unable to connect with many birth relatives, I try to focus on the miracles in my life when the pain gets to me. I understand that Michelle and my aunts on Jeffrey's side might have a hard time accepting my existence. They are undoubtedly going through a period where they are unsure of how to fit me into their lives. The miracle here is that I don't sit around and wait for them to call anymore. I don't have time to pine away for relatives who I really don't know, hoping that they will someday offer me a tidbit of time in their lives. When I start to get down on myself, it helps to remind myself of what I do have: many people love me, my career brings immeasurable meaning and purpose to my life, I adore my friends, I have a wonderful soul mate, and a beautiful relationship with Liz.

After almost two years of estrangement from my adoptive mother, I decided to bite the bullet and call her. From all my work in writing this book and in counseling, I knew that the only way for me to continue to heal my relationships is to forgive and forget. It seemed that the last major unresolved relationship in my life was with my adoptive mother. Even though I was angry at her and even though she had made mistakes, I was grieving the loss of our relationship nonetheless. I knew that I would be willing to have contact with her again, but under very different circumstances and with definite emotional boundaries. I was sure that over the last two years she thought of me quite often, if not every day. She might even have missed me, as I missed having a mother-daughter relationship. She might have been waiting for me to call her, hoping that I would. I also knew that I couldn't just wait around for her to make the first move and contact me. We are both very stubborn when it comes to hurt feelings.

As far as I knew, she still lived in South Carolina. Since directory assistance had been helpful in the past, I decided to give it a shot. What did I have to lose? It was a Tuesday evening in late November of 1999 when I located her number in Mayesville, South Carolina. I debated over when to call: Should I call her now, 9:00 p.m. her time, or wait until tomorrow morning? All I knew for sure was that I was going to call her eventually. Why not now? Why not get it over with? Find out what the story is instead of spending another minute wasting my energy trying to figure out what I did wrong, if anything.

I dialed the number; it was 6:07 p.m. my time. One

ring, two, then three. On the fourth ring my adoptive mother answered. I had the right number.

I got right down to business. I explained the reason for my call and that I wanted to clear the air after almost two years of not speaking to each other. She was very pleased to hear from me and exclaimed over and over again how pleased she was to hear my voice. I believed her. I told her I was glad to hear her voice as well. I meant it. We hashed out the last few conversations before our estrangement, and not surprisingly, we had very different perceptions of what happened back in December of 1997. I recounted how my feelings were hurt when she didn't take my word regarding the sunglasses incident. She listened to everything I had to say and then it was her turn.

She was under the impression that I was angry with her, but she didn't know why. She did not remember hanging up on me, but she was sure that she had done something wrong that led me to not say good-bye to her before she moved across the country. Little did she know how angry I was with her. I was able to explain to her why I was so upset with her and she was able to apologize to me. It was wonderful to tell her how I felt and to clear the air. I never thought I would talk to her again and now we were having a civil, if not loving conversation as if we had never been estranged. I understand now that each person perceives the same situation differently.

We ended up on the phone for one and a half hours. She talked about South Carolina and her dogs.

She talked about Peter and his wife and about Todd. For the first time I was able to listen to my mother talk about Todd and understand that she loves all her children, and that includes Todd. I cannot expect her to not talk about him during our conversations. She asked how I was doing, and I updated her on my life and told her that I had written a book about my experiences of growing up adopted. I was so pleased to hear that she has in fact read many books on adoption and was surprisingly receptive to the idea of me writing my story. She said she understood how both of us may have misinterpreted what happened in my childhood, but that her reading of various books on adoption has helped her to better understand me, the adoptee in her life. I explained that while I perceived some things as having gone dreadfully wrong in my childhood, it was now obvious to me, and hopefully would be to her too if she decided to read my book, that the strengths she had given me helped me triumph over my vulnerabilities. I was finally able to thank her for all she did give me and to tell her that thanks to her and the other members of my adoption triangle, I am a fully functioning and competent adult.

Bottom line is that I took another risk. I told my adoptive mother how I felt about her treatment of me and now I am in contact with her again. After I hung up I collected some pictures of my basenjis and mailed them off to her. When she received them she called and thanked me again for getting in touch with her. I am looking forward to a mutually satisfying relationship with my adoptive mother, all the while knowing that we will always have our own perception of what happened when I was growing up. I will no longer strive to be the good daughter, just a good person who wants to hear how her mother is doing. I am striving to not have any expectations of the relationship, because expectations lead to disappointment. Who knows, maybe I will take her up on her invitation to visit her in Mayesville someday. You never know!

My adoptive father and I have a great relationship today. We live about twenty miles apart and talk on the phone often. We don't always agree on what happened when I was growing up, but he accepts my feelings and perceptions about it, which I appreciate. As you have read, my once emotionally distant adoptive father and I haven't always had a great relationship, but I'm happy to report that we are now very close. We have gone through the full spectrum of the father-daughter relationship. As a child, I ran to him when I felt my adoptive mother was mean to me, and I hated him for not protecting me from Todd, but now I can honestly say that I love him with all my heart. He is truly able to see me as a separate individual and he supports my dreams and goals. He threw me a dinner party to meet my birth relatives, and a graduation party to celebrate the completion of my master's degree. He's truly become my father in every sense of the word. Only a blood bond could make us closer.

He and my stepmother, Kimberly, have always treated me well. In fact, Kimberly has become more the main mother figure in my life. I appreciate her for loving my father, but also for the way she loves me as if I were her real daughter. I realized recently that I hadn't made amends to her for the time I told her not to come to my college graduation because my adoptive mother refused to attend if she did. I had no idea how much that must have hurt her. I do now. I assured her that I would never let my adoptive mother manipulate me like that ever again. Kimberly means too much to me to ever hurt her again.

The last time I saw my adoptive father, I asked him about the process of adopting me and about the time surrounding the abuse by Todd. Not surprisingly, the agency never told him I would miss my birth mother. He didn't know when I cried around my birthday that he could have recognized it as a sign that I missed Vanessa. He never knew what to do, that he could have knelt down and taken me in his arms and attempted to console me. It's not his fault. He was ill-informed.

In a recent conversation, my adoptive father became very upset to learn that Todd continued to molest me after returning from jail. He did not know because I did not tell him. He reminded me how he took immediate action the first time I told him about the molestation, and I've never forgotten that. He asked me why I never told him when it happened the second time, and I explained that I feared Todd would kill me. Whether he really would have done it is irrelevant. He scared me, and fear is a powerful mechanism. Basically, since my adoptive father never knew, I couldn't blame him anymore. It was very healing to have this discussion, and he reassured me that had I told him that Todd continued to abuse me, he would have sent him away for good.

Needless to say, Todd and I haven't spoken since he moved out of the house when I was sixteen years old. I saw him at Elizabeth's funeral, but purposely avoided contact with him, mourned the loss of my beloved grandmother, and left the cemetery knowing that I would not ever have to see him again if I didn't want to. A few years back, Todd started sending me literature describing a cult that he had gotten involved in. I wrote him a letter requesting that he stop sending me materials since I was not interested. I also used this letter as an opportunity to address the molestation. I wrote how I was working on forgiving him, how the forgiveness comes and goes, but that I would never forget what happened. I also made it perfectly clear that I did not ever want a relationship with him. Fortunately, he admitted what he'd done. I realize that many people refuse to admit their actions, but he didn't. For that I am eternally grateful. He actually wrote me back and apologized for what he could only refer to as his "transgressions." I keep his letter as a reminder.

As I continue to process my feelings and the abusive situation with Todd, I can't help but wonder if maybe Todd and Peter were adversely affected by my adoption as well. Were they mad at me for entering the family and taking Mom's attention away? Was the attempted drowning incident an act of jealous revenge on Todd's part? Was he trying to get rid of me as the source of Mom's distraction? Did he molest me because he desperately needed love from Mom and Dad? These are questions that I needed to ask myself in order to help put some valuable perspective on what happened. Again, it doesn't excuse what happened by a long shot, it just helps resolve the pain and confusion as to why things went horribly wrong. I can say with certainty that he obviously was a very troubled child.

Peter still lives in South Carolina, and I can safely say that we have no relationship. Of course, we never really did. After all, we had nothing in common and nothing to talk about. We share the same birthday, but only by coincidence. There our similarities end. He lives close to my adoptive mother, though, and I'm glad he's there for her. I do hope he is happy.

I now realize that reunion only begins a new life. I also recognize the healing process for what it is—a process, nothing more, nothing less. The pain and feelings will continue to exist under the surface, but if I continue in my endeavors, I'm confident my life will continue to get exponentially better.

The people you have read about in this book are real, regardless of the fact that I have changed their names. Whether my experience with any of them has been good or bad, I have learned much from every moment we spent together. I have healed immensely in ways I never would have thought possible.

Despite what any adoption agency paperwork has ever said, I know my initial relinquishment affected me profoundly. As you have read, I continually deal with the repercussions of a decision made a lifetime ago. Everyone heals differently, and I have only revealed here the path that I took, the one that led to my ability to forgive and accept the people and situations in my life.

Being found by my birth family is one of the greatest things that ever happened to me, and I thank the universe every day for this beautiful gift. As the result of my reunion, I have truly been able to find myself. My journey through reunion continues to bring me joy, and opportunities to heal and let go. All persons in my family tree, both birth and adoptive, help identify me, and give me roots and purpose in a world where I never quite knew how I fit in. I hope that all adoptees can experience this feeling someday.

Appendix

KASEY'S FAVORITE QUOTES

"[The aftermath of adoption is] something that can lie dormant most of one's life. If it erupts in childhood, adolescence, or early adulthood and is dismissed as neurotic behavior or normal rebellion, it can subside into numbness. But it can stir malignantly in some adoptees all their lives, making them detached, floating, unable to love or to trust: loners."
BETTY JEAN LIFTON, AUTHOR OF *TWICE BORN*

"The truth of his [or her] origin is the birthright of every man [or woman]."
FLORENCE FISHER, PRESIDENT AND FOUNDER OF THE ADOPTEE'S LIBERTY MOVEMENT ASSOCIATION (ALMA)

"If you do not know your past, you can't know the future."
ERIC ERIKSON, FELLOW ADOPTEE

"Help! I am being help prisoner by my heredity and environment."
DENNIS ALLEN

"Truth hurts—not the searching after, the running from."
JOHN EYBERG

ATTENTION MEMBERS OF THE
ADOPTION COMMUNITY!

(and those who love us)

I am currently working on my next book, which will delve into the main issues that affect the various members of the adoption community and will describe how they worked through them to a resolution. I will be dividing the book into sections. I will take each topic and investigate the issue, then offer hope and suggestions on how to work through it. I want your input.

Here are some suggested topics. Feel free to add other issues that you feel are pertinent.

Depression; Self-sabotage; Substance Abuse;
Anger; Fear of Intimacy; Difficulty in Bonding;
Difficulty in Trusting; Fear of Abandonment;
Relationship Difficulties;
Co-dependency; Guilt; Shame.

Please answer all that apply to your past and/or current situation:

1. Adoption Community Members:

   a. What is the main issue or difficulty in your life?

   b. What strategies do you employ to help you work through the pain and come to a resolution? *over→*

    c. What has worked and what has not
worked for you, and why?

2. Significant Others:

    a. What are the main issues that you observe
in the adoption community member in
your life?

    b. How do you deal with those issues?

3. Mental Health Professionals:

    a. In your practice, what recurring issues
are you presented with as you serve
members of the adoption community?

    b. What tools and strategies do you offer
to lead them to resolutions?

Please send your descriptions to Kasey Hamner at:

Mail: Triad Publishing
       P.O. Box 8514
       La Crescenta, CA 91224-0514

Fax: (818) 957-5526

Email: healingheart@earthlink.net

Also state whether or not you will allow me to
include your input, with names and identifying
information altered, in my next book.

Thank you in advance.

Order Form for *Whose Child?* by Kasey Hamner

Title	Quantity	Price	Subtotal
Whose Child? ISBN: 0-9674145-0-4		$14.95 each	$
CA residents: add $1.23 sales tax per copy.			$
Shipping/Handling: add $3.50 for first copy, $1.00 each additional.			$
		TOTAL:	$

Bulk Order Discounts: 5-9 books-20%; 10-99 books-40% and free shipping; 100+-50% and free shipping.
bulk order discounts apply to book price only, not to sales tax or shipping/handling.

ONLINE: http://www.bookzone.com/bookzone/10001914.html
EMAIL: healingheart@earthlink.net
PHONE/FAX: (818) 957-5526
MAIL ORDER: Triad Publishing, P.O. Box 8514,
La Crescenta, CA 91224-0514

____ **Check enclosed** (mail orders only, payable to Triad Publishing, U.S. Funds Only)

____ **Please bill my Credit Card**

____Mastercard ____Visa ____American Express

Credit Card Number: _____

Expiration Date: _____

Name: _____

Ship to Address: _____

_____

Telephone: Day:_____ Evening: _____

Email Address: _____

Check all that apply:___adoptee ___birth parent ___ adoptive parent

___M.F.T. ___Clinical Psychologist ___Social Worker___ Counselor

___Other (please specify)_____

Visit Triad Publishing's Web Site: http://home.earthlink.net/~healingheart

Order Form for *Whose Child?* by Kasey Hamner

Title	Quantity	Price	Subtotal
Whose Child? ISBN: 0-9674145-0-4		$14.95 each	$
CA residents: add $1.23 sales tax per copy.			$
Shipping/Handling: add $3.50 for first copy, $1.00 each additional.			$
		TOTAL:	$

Bulk Order Discounts: 5-9 books-20%; 10-99 books-40% and free shipping; 100+-50% and free shipping. bulk order discounts apply to book price only, not to sales tax or shipping/handling.

ONLINE: http://www.bookzone.com/bookzone/10001914.html
EMAIL: healingheart@earthlink.net
PHONE/FAX: (818) 957-5526
MAIL ORDER: Triad Publishing, P.O. Box 8514, La Crescenta, CA 91224-0514

____ **Check enclosed** (mail orders only, payable to Triad Publishing, U.S. Funds Only)

____ **Please bill my Credit Card**

____Mastercard ____Visa ____American Express

Credit Card Number: _____

Expiration Date: _____

Name: _____

Ship to Address: _____

_____

Telephone: Day:_____ Evening: _____

Email Address: _____

Check all that apply:___adoptee ___birth parent ___ adoptive parent

___M.F.T. ___Clinical Psychologist ___Social Worker___ Counselor

___Other (please specify)_____

Visit Triad Publishing's Web Site: http://home.earthlink.net/~healingheart